VAN LILL'S
SOUTH AFRICAN
MISCELLANY

❧ ❦ ❧

VAN LILL'S
SOUTH AFRICAN
MISCELLANY

❧ ❧ ❧

❧ ❧ ❧

Dawid van Lill

ZEBRA

Published by Zebra Press
an imprint of Struik Publishers
(a division of New Holland Publishing (South Africa) (Pty) Ltd)
PO Box 1144, Cape Town, 8000
New Holland Publishing is a member of Johnnic Communications Ltd

www.zebrapress.co.za

First published 2004

1 3 5 7 9 10 8 6 4 2

Publication © Zebra Press 2004
Text © Dawid van Lill 2004

Cover illustrations: David du Plessis
Other illustrations: Stephen Bankart

PUBLISHING MANAGER: Marlene Fryer
MANAGING EDITOR: Robert Plummer
EDITOR: Ronel Richter-Herbert
COVER AND TEXT DESIGNER: Natascha Adendorff
TYPESETTER: Natascha Adendorff
PRODUCTION CONTROLLER: Valerie Kommer

Set in Adobe Garamond

Reproduction by Hirt & Carter (Cape) (Pty) Ltd
Printed and bound by Paarl Print, Oosterland Street, Paarl, South Africa

ISBN 1 86872 921 4

www.imagesofafrica.co.za
IMAGES OF AFRICA
PHOTO LIBRARY

I like to know things. Not everything about everything, but as much as I can about anything. Who, what, where, when and why frequently enter my thoughts, and that's why I jumped at the idea of compiling a South African miscellany. True to my nature, I just had to know where the word *miscellany* comes from. According to my collection of dictionaries, a miscellany is a collection of many different things or kinds of things that do not necessarily have any connection whatsoever. The word *miscellany* comes from the late 16th century, via the French word *miscellanées* from the Latin *miscellanea*, and, ultimately, from *miscere*, which means *to mix*. It also has quite a number of synonyms: assortment, collection, selection, grouping, medley, pastiche, variety, diversity, hotchpotch, jumble, mixed bag, mishmash, mixture ...

I am inquisitive by nature. Always have been, always will be – guess that's just part of my nature. Facts, trivia and statistics have always fascinated me. Maybe it has something to do with the fact that I had to rely on books, magazines, newspapers and the radio to provide me with all the information I needed when I was growing up. There was no TV, PC, PS2 or WWW at the time – a fact that my own kids can't comprehend at all! It forced me to read, read, read, and listen (in that order and ratio).

So there you have it. This book is a mixture of facts and trivia that I find interesting and fascinating. It is *not* an encyclopaedia or a comprehensive handbook of facts about South Africa, although I have tried to include as many of the relevant facts as I could find about any given subject in the book. Many of the subjects have been included because I wanted to know more about them, could not find an easily accessible source, and started to dig. An example: I wondered what the petrol price had been in 1990, and how it has increased over the past 14 years. And what about the gold price? Or the rand–dollar exchange rate? Not to mention the repo rate. And what *is* the repo rate? We know the Big Five mammals, but what about the Big Six of the bird world? Or the Big Twelve of insects? Which South Africans have won gold medals at the Olympic Games? How do our earthquakes compare to the world's large tremors? Which South Africans played test rugby for other countries? And so it goes on and on and on. That is why my motto is, 'Insatiable curiosity is a thousand times better than terminal ignorance.'

One of the pitfalls in compiling collections of trivia and miscellaneous information is that mistakes are bound to creep in. We have done everything we could to eliminate the little 'expletive deleteds', but errors are very persistent beasts. I did my very best to keep to the fact, the whole fact, and nothing but the fact, but to err is, unfortunately, all too human. Any mistake is bound to be all mine! There won't be a big prize for finding errors, so please don't pull a brain muscle in an effort to find any …

The facts used in the book were collected (and checked) until the end of August 2004. Any changes that happened afterwards will, unfortunately, not be reflected in this edition.

As with all rather haphazard collections of trivia compiled by an individual with specific fields of interest, you might miss a number of your favourite categories and interesting facts in *Van Lill's South African Miscellany*. Please don't feel aggrieved if your specific interest is not mentioned, even in passing – rather do something about it! Let me know what you would like to see in a next book (sequels are quite popular these days), give me a clue or two about the whereabouts of said info, and I will consider it. Regard this as an interactive work in progress, to which you are very welcome to contribute. My e-mail address is: satrivia@iknow.co.za.

One question that I am asked very often is: 'Where on earth did you get that information?' The short answer is: 'I dig for it!' I have used thousands of sources to find, check and verify the facts in this book. If you want to know more about any subject, please have a look at the bibliography. I've used literally thousands of sources, and I have included the most important source for each category. The Internet plays a much bigger role in our lives than a few years ago, and you'll notice quite a number of Internet addresses. If you go to the addresses listed there, you'll find all the information that you are looking for.

Lastly, a word of thanks to the people who helped to keep me honest and the book as error-free as possible. First and foremost my wife, Marina, whose positive criticism always leads to better books. Marlene Fryer first approached me with the idea for the book, and Robert Plummer looked at the half-finished product, suggested all the necessary changes and additions, shuffled things around like a seasoned magician and had a big hand in polishing the final product. Ronel Richter-Herbert dotted the i's and crossed the t's, and kept all the other letters of the alphabet in place. It is an author's dream to entrust a book like this to such a dedicated team.

DAWID VAN LILL
CAPE TOWN 2004

——— SOUTH AFRICA'S FAUNA AND FLORA ———

'A wealth of animal life exists in the region. [South Africa] hosts an estimated 5,8% of the world's total mammal species, 8% of bird species, 4,6% of the global diversity of reptile species, 16% of the total number of marine fish species, and 5,5% of the world's classified insect species.'

— *South Africa Yearbook 2003/04*

Fauna was an ancient Italian rural goddess, the sister of Faunus. **Flora**, also of Roman origin, was the goddess of flowers and springtime. She even had a festival – the Floralia, a spirited affair with dramatic spectacles, including animal hunts, at the famous Circus Maximus. Flora is generally depicted as a beautiful maiden, with a garland of flowers.

South Africa is …

… the third most biologically diverse country in the world.

… the only country on Earth to have an entire plant kingdom within its national borders.

… the 24th richest country in the world, and the 5th richest in Africa, in terms of the number of mammal, bird, reptile and amphibian species that occur only in this country ('endemics').

South Africa has …

… about 18 000 vascular plant species within its boundaries, of which 80% are found nowhere else.

… one-third of the world's succulent plant species.

The Cape Floral Kingdom …

… has the highest recorded species diversity for any similar-sized temperate or tropical region in the world.

… is the world's 'hottest hotspot' of global conservation concern. A 'hotspot' is an area where high levels of species richness, endemism and threat coincide.

——— SOUTH AFRICA'S SPECIES RICHNESS ———

Species	Described species	Percentage of Earth's species
Mammals	295	5,8
Birds	951	8,0
Amphibians	84	2,1
Reptiles	286	4,6
Freshwater fish	112	1,3
Marine fish	2 150	16,0
Invertebrates	77 500	5,5
Vascular plants	18 625	7,5

≈ NUMBER OF SPECIES PER PROVINCE ≈

Province	Biome	Veld type	Plant	Mammal	Bird	Amphibian	Reptile
Eastern Cape	6	29	6 383	156	384	51	57
Free State	3	19	3 001	93	334	29	47
Gauteng	2	9	2 826	125	326	25	53
KwaZulu-Natal	3	19	5 515	177	462	68	86
Limpopo	2	14	4 239	239	479	44	89
Mpumalanga	2	20	4 593	160	464	48	82
Northern Cape	4	20	4 916	139	302	29	53
North West	2	10	2 483	138	384	27	59
Western Cape	6	19	9 489	153	305	39	52

≈ CONSERVATION OF SOUTH AFRICAN BIOMES ≈

Biome	Vegetation types	Percentage of South Africa	Percentage conserved in South Africa
Forest	3	0,59	17,90
Fynbos	5	3,39	20,25
Renosterveld	5	2,90	1,67
Grassland	15	24,46	2,52
Nama-Karoo	6	24,41	0,57
Succulent	4	6,77	2,82
Savannah	25	34,24	10,15
Thicket	5	3,44	4,50

SOUTH AFRICA'S NATIONAL PARKS

Park	Proclaimed	Area 1994 (ha)	Added since 1994 (ha)	Current size (ha)
Addo Elephant	1931	51 309	23 030	74 339
Agulhas	1999	0	5 690	5 690
Augrabies Falls	1966	11 743	29 933	41 676
Bontebok	1931	2 786	0	2 786
Table Mountain*	1998	0	22 100	22 100
Golden Gate Highlands	1963	11 633	0	11 633
Kalahari Gemsbok**	1931	959 103	0	959 103
Karoo	1979	41 047	36 047	77 094
Knysna National Lakes Area	1985	15 000	0	15 000
Kruger	1926	1 962 362	0	1 962 362
Marakele	1993	37 035	13 691	50 726
Mountain Zebra	1937	6 536	18 127	24 633
Richtersveld	1991	162 445	0	162 445
Tankwa-Karoo	1986	27 064	16 835	43 899
Tsitsikamma	1964	63 942	0	63 942
Vaalbos	1986	22 697	0	22 697
Mapungubwe***	1998	0	5 356	5 356
West Coast	1985	32 361	3 912	36 273
Wilderness	1985	10 600	0	10 600
Total				**3 592 354**

*   Previously known as Cape Peninsula National Park
** Now part of the Kgalagadi Transfrontier Park
***Previously known as the Vhembe-Dongola National Park

SOUTH AFRICA'S TRANSFRONTIER CONSERVATION AREAS

Name	Total area (km²)	Area (km²)		
		South Africa	Other countries (1)	Other countries (2)
Ai-Ais/Richtersveld Transfrontier Conservation Park	6 222	1 902 (31%)	4 320 in Namibia (69%)	
Kgalagadi Transfrontier Park (KTP)	37 991	9 591 (27%)	28 400 in Botswana (73%)	
Limpopo-Shashe Transfrontier Conservation Area	4 872	2 561 (53%)	1 350 in Botswana (28%)	960 in Zimbabwe (19%)
Great Limpopo Transfrontier Park	35 000	20 300 (58%)	8 400 in Mozambique (24%)	6 300 in Zimbabwe (18%)
Lubombo Transfrontier Conservation and Resource Area	4 195	1 095 (26%)	317 in Swaziland (8%)	2 783 in Mozambique (66%)
Maloti–Drakensberg Transfrontier Conservation and Development Area	8 113	2 943 (36%)	5 170 in Lesotho (64%)	

GESTATION PERIODS OF
SOME SOUTH AFRICAN MAMMALS

Mammal	Days	Mammal	Days
Mouse (domestic white)	19	Sheep (domestic)	144–151
Mouse (meadow)	21	Goat (domestic)	145–155
Hedgehog	30	Vervet monkey	165
Rabbit (domestic)	30–35	Baboon	187
Mole	35	Aardvark	210
Squirrel (grey)	30–40	Hippopotamus	225–250
Cat (domestic)	58–65	Otter	270–300
Dog (domestic)	58–70	Cow	279–292
Guinea pig	68	Seal	330
Warthog	72	Horse	330–342
African wild dog	72	Dolphin	350
Leopard	92–95	Donkey	365
Cheetah	95	Zebra (Grant's)	365
Hyena	93	Giraffe	420–450
Lion	108	Rhinoceros (black)	450
Porcupine	112	Whale (sperm)	480–500
Pig (domestic)	112–115		

ALL CREATURES GREAT AND SMALL

South Africa has an abundance of wildlife, but one of the most interesting features of the local animals is the record size they reach – large as well as small.

Record	Animal	Scientific name	Height/Length/Speed	Weight
Largest land mammal	African elephant	*Loxodonta Africana*	3,50 m (height)	6 tons (male)
Largest fish	Whale shark	*Rhincodon typus*	12,65 m (length)	15–21 tons
Tallest mammal	Giraffe	*Giraffa camelopardalis*	5,3 m (height)	
Fastest land mammal	Cheetah	*Acinonyx jubatus*	112 km/h (speed)	
Fastest bird	Peregrine falcon	*Falco peregrinus*	250–380 km/h (speed)	
Largest antelope	Derby eland	*Taurotragus derbianus*	1,8 m tall (shoulder)	700 kg (male)
Heaviest flying bird	Kori bustard	*Ardeotis kori*	120–150 cm (length)	13,5–19 kg
Largest wingspan	Wandering albatross	*Diomedea exulans*	3,63 m (length)	
Largest bird	Ostrich	*Struthio camelus*	2,40 m (height)	156,5 kg
Smallest chelonian	Speckled Cape tortoise	*Homopus signatus*	6 cm–9,6 cm (length)	

Did you know?

- The most efficient scavenger is the spotted hyena (*Crocuta crocuta*), which is the only animal with a digestive system that can break down bones, hooves, horns and hides.
- The most abundant bird is a seed-eating weaver, the redbilled Quelea (*Quelea quelea*), which has an estimated breeding population of 1,5 billion. Every year 200 million are killed – and it doesn't even make the slightest dent in their numbers.

THE BIG FIVE

Name	Black rhino (Hook-lipped rhino) White rhino (Square-lipped rhino)	Lion	Leopard	Elephant	Buffalo
Scientific name	*Diceros bicornis* *Ceratotherium simum*	*Panthera leo*	*Panthera pardus*	*Loxodonta Africana*	*Syncerus caffer*
Height	150 cm at shoulder	± 100 cm	± 60 cm	± 3,50 m	165 cm at shoulder
Mass	1 to 1½ tons (hook-lipped rhino) Over 2 tons (square-lipped rhino)	Male: 180–240 kg; Female: 120–180 kg	20–82 kg 17–35 kg	± 5 500– 6 000 kg ± 3 600– 4 000 kg	± 680–750 kg
Lifespan	35 to 40 years	± 20 years	21 years in captivity	60 to 70 years	20 years
Habitat	Grassland and open savannahs	Grassy plains and open woodlands	Bush and riverine forest	Dense forest to open plains	Dense forest to open plains
Diet	Herbivorous	Meat	Carnivorous	Herbivorous	Herbivorous/ grazer
Gestation	16 months (white rhino)	± 3½ months	± 2½ months	± 22 months	11–12 months
Predators	Humans	Humans	Lion, crocodile, humans	Humans	Humans and lions

THE BIG SIX

The Big Six are some of South Africa's most majestic birds.

Name	Kori bustard	Martial eagle	Saddlebilled stork	Ground hornbill	Lappetfaced vulture	Pel's fishing owl
Scientific name	*Ardeotis Kori*	*Polemaetus bellicosus*	*Ephippiorhynchus senegalensis*	*Bucorvus leadbeateri*	*Torgos tracheliotus*	*Scotopeloa peli*
Afrikaans	Gompou	Breëkop- arend	Saalbek- ooievaar	Bromvoël	Swartaasvoël	Visuil
Length	120–150 cm	78–83 cm	145 cm	90–129 cm	98–105 cm	63 cm
Breeding	Oct–Feb	April–June	March–July	Oct–Nov	April–July	Jan–June
Eggs	2 eggs	1 egg	1–2 eggs	1–2 eggs	1 egg	2 eggs
Incubation	27–30 days	47–51 days	33 days	40 days	56 days	33–38 days
RDB status	Vulnerable	Vulnerable	Rare	Vulnerable	Vulnerable	Rare

Kori bustard

The Kori bustard is a very large bird, with greyish-brown upper parts and a white belly. In the breeding season it is either solitary or in pairs, and in groups of 40 birds during the rest of the year. It eats carrion, seeds, small vertebrates, insects and the Acacia gum, which gave it its Afrikaans name. The male displays with his white neck feathers inflated, and his tail raised to expose the white underparts of the tail feathers. It makes a deep 'vum vum' sound when it takes off, and is a strong flyer.

Martial eagle

The martial eagle is a dark-brown bird with a white belly with black streaks, and white legs with very large yellow talons. It is a common bird throughout South Africa, and usually lives in areas with suitable trees. This eagle hunts from perches or from the air, and eats other birds, reptiles and even small mammals, such as hares and dassies, and antelope, such as impala and grey duikers. Its nest is large (2 m in diameter and 2 m thick) and lined with leaves. The father provides the food, and the mother feeds the chicks.

Saddlebilled stork

The saddlebilled stork is a large black and white bird with very long legs, and an enormous, slightly upturned red and black bill, with a yellow 'saddle'. It has a naked red patch on the breast, and its neck and head are all black. The adult birds are silent. Saddlebilled storks live in the north-eastern parts of South Africa near inland water, such as swamps, pans, dams and rivers. It is a solitary bird, which feeds in shallow water, and stirs the mud with its feet. It stabs its prey with its bill, and throws it into the air before swallowing it. This stork is carnivorous, and eats fish and frogs, as well as small mammals. Its nest is in a tree, and consists of a large platform, 50 cm thick and with a diameter of 2 m.

Ground hornbill

The ground hornbill is black, with white tail feathers and red faces and red throat wattles, with a bluish part on the female's throat. It can be found in pairs or groups of not more than eight in open grassy areas, savannah and woodland. It digs with its bill for food, and is quite vocal. It flies powerfully, with deep wing beats. It is carnivorous, and eats reptiles, snails, frogs, insects and mammals as big as hares. The female's nest is in a hole in a tree, which is lined with leaves and grass. The opening is about 40 cm wide, and, unlike other hornbills, the male does not seal her in.

Lappetfaced vulture

The lappetfaced vulture is a very large black bird, with black and white streaked underparts. It has a large reddish head and a heavy bill. It is usually silent, and lives in the north-eastern parts of South Africa, in savannah and desert environments. It can be seen solitary or in pairs, and spends its nights in a tree. It eats carrion, and can eat tougher material than other vultures. It is usually the dominant vulture at a carcass. Its nest is large and can have a diameter of up to 3 m, and a depth of 50 to 100 cm. It consists of sticks, which are lined with skin, hair and grass. Both sexes incubate the eggs.

Pel's fishing owl

Pel's fishing owl is a large bird without ear tufts, and its tawny rufous upper parts are streaked with black. Its belly is tawny buff, with black streaks. It has a large head and eyes, and makes a deep hooting sound. It can be found in suitable habitats near water, usually in pairs or groups of three birds. Pel's fishing owls are night birds, and they rest in shady trees during the day. They eat mainly fish (as much as 2 kg per day) and other water creatures, such as mussels, crabs and frogs, and even young crocodiles. The claws are adapted to catch slippery prey – it has spiny soles and long claws. They nest in a hollow in a tree, fairly high above the ground.

───────────── THE BIG TWELVE ─────────────

A Big Five for the mammals … A Big Six for the Birds … A Super 12 for rugby players … Why not a Big Twelve for the insect world? After all, there *are* some impressive specimens in South Africa. The innovative Big Twelve Insect Project is supported by the Entomological Society of Southern Africa, the Transvaal Museum and the Durban Museum.

	Insect	Scientific name	Order	Description
1	Giant dragonfly	*Anax tristis*	Odonata	The giant dragonfly is longer than 110 mm and has a wingspan in excess of 133 mm. It is found in the east of Zimbabwe, and can fly very fast. South Africa's largest dragonfly is *Anax speratus*, with a wingspan of more than 120 mm. Adult dragonflies eat anything they can catch.
2	Table Mountain flightless cockroach	*Aptera fusca*	Blattodea	This cockroach is quite large – more than 36 mm long. The females are wingless, but the males have wings and can fly. The female gives birth to live young, which she carries around with her for a while.

	Insect	Scientific name	Order	Description
3	Termite	*Marcoterms species*	Isoptera	Termites are impressive architects and builders, and some of the mounds they build can be higher than 2 m. They are also ecologically important, recycling nutrients and aerating the soil.
4	Bladder grasshopper	*Pneumora species*	Orthoptera	Most of the bladder grasshoppers are endemic to South Africa, and are well known for the sounds they produce by rubbing their hind legs against files on their abdomens. This inflated 'bladder' (hence the name) resonates to produce the spectacular sound. The males can fly, but the females are flightless.
5	Giant stick insect	*Bactrododema tiaratum*	Phasmatodea	This is a huge insect, and the female can measure 125–185 mm. They have small wings, but can fly or glide downwards. Because they move slowly and live high in trees, they have to conserve water, and have specially adapted blood or haemolymph to achieve this.
6	Giant praying mantis	*Ischnomantis fatilogua*	Mantodea	The praying mantis is everything but peaceful, despite its name. It is a fierce predator, and can catch a fly in flight with its modified front legs. *Ischnomantis fatilogua* can be longer than 130 mm.
7	Giant water bug	*Lethocerus cordofanus*	Heteroptera	Small fish and tadpoles form part of this aquatic predator's diet. It doesn't use dissolved oxygen like dragonflies, but breathes surface oxygen through its tail, which is modified to act like a snorkel. The largest specimen (in the Transvaal museum) is 78 mm long and 30,2 mm wide.
8	Giant antlion	*Palpares immensus*	Neuroptera	Antlion pits are well known to children all over the country, but the adult insect, which looks very much like a dragonfly, is not earthbound. It has a wingspan of 127 mm, and is a strong flier.
9	Giant tachinid fly	*Dejeania bombylans*	Diptera	These insects are parasites, and are quite common in South Africa, although they don't favour Cape Town and the western parts of South Africa.
10	Giant dung beetle	*Heliocopris andersoni*	Coleoptera	The dung beetle is a fascinating insect. It is quite large – 57 mm long and 33 mm wide – and has a wingspan of more than 135 mm. They recycle dung by breaking it up, and some of these insects have even been exported to Australia for this purpose. The female dung beetle lays her eggs in a ball of dung (which

	Insect	Scientific name	Order	Description
				can be 10,3 mm in diameter), and the young use the dung as food until they emerge.
11	Mopane worm	*Imbrasia belina*	Lepidoptera	The edible mopane worm has become a household name in the northern provinces of South Africa, because of its commercial possibilities. This caterpillar is named after the mopane tree on which it feeds.
12	Giant carpenter bee	*Xylocopa flavorufa*	Hymenoptera	These bees make their nests by hollowing out dry plant tissue. They pollinate crops and indigenous plants, and feed their young a mixture of pollen and nectar. The carpenter bee is fairly large, and has a wingspan of 63 mm, and a body length of up to 30 mm.

Did you know?

- The largest insect ever known was a *Meganeura monyi*, a prehistoric dragonfly, which lived about 280 000 000 years ago. It had a wingspan of up to 70 cm.
- The largest known stick insect, Borneo's *Phobaeticus kirbyi*, is also the longest insect in the world. The female can reach a length of 328 mm.

THE CRADLE OF HUMANKIND

- The Cradle of Humankind is a 47 000-ha area in the Sterkfontein Valley, 50 km west of Johannesburg, where three million years of human activity have taken place.
- 40% of the world's human ancestor fossils have been found in this region.
- These sites produced the remains of hominids (human and pre-human) from over 2 to 3,5 million years ago, from the early Stone Age, middle Stone Age, later Stone Age, and the early and late Iron Age up to today.
- The Sterkfontein cave is the best-known site, where over 500 hominid fossils and more than 9 000 stone tools have been found.

Major finds		
Discovery	Discovered by	Year
The fossil of Mrs Ples (now believed to be a Master Ples), an *Australopithecus africanus* that dates back 2,5 million years.	Robert Broom	1947
Little Foot, an almost complete apeman skeleton, is 3,3 million years old.	Ronald Clarke and Phillip Tobias	1995
An almost complete hominid skeleton, dating back 3,5 million years. The complete skull and fragments of arm, foot and leg bones have been uncovered so far.	Ronald Clarke	1998

There are about 40 different fossil sites in the Sterkfontein Valley, and 13 have been excavated. These include:

Site	Discovery
Bolts Farm	The remains of three sabre-tooth cats, found in a pit that trapped animals
Haasgat	The fossils of early forest-dwelling monkeys
Swartkrans	The site of the earliest known deliberate use of fire, about 1,3 million years ago
Gondolin	90 000 fossil specimens, found here since 1979

- The Sterkfontein Valley landscape consists of a number of important palaeo-anthropological sites, namely Sterkfontein, Kromdraai, Coopers B, Wonder Cave, Drimolen, Gladysvale, Plover's Lake and Minnaar's Caves.
- The Cradle of Humankind was once, some 2,5 billion years ago, a shallow inland sea, but the water evaporated over time and the mud formed dolomite rock.
- Mohale's Gate, 8 km from the Sterkfontein cave, which has seven 20-m tall concrete monoliths, will eventually become the hub of the whole Cradle of Humankind site.

—— SOUTH AFRICA'S WORLD HERITAGE SITES ——

- South Africa ratified the World Heritage Convention in May 1997. The South Africa World Heritage Convention Committee identifies possible sites in South Africa. Cultural and natural sites in South Africa can be granted World Heritage status according to the World Heritage Convention Act, 1999 (Act 49 of 1999).
- The following sites have been proclaimed World Heritage Sites by the United Nations Educational, Scientific and Cultural Organisation (UNESCO):
  - Robben Island (1999)
  - The uKhahlamba-Drakensberg Park (1999)
  - Mapungubwe cultural landscape (2003)
  - The hominid sites at Swartkrans, Sterkfontein and Kromdraai (which are known as the Cradle of Humankind)
  - The Greater St Lucia Wetland Park (1999)
  - Cape Floral Region Protected Areas (2004)
- In July 2004 there were 788 World Heritage Sites – 154 natural sites, 611 cultural sites, and 23 mixed sites. The four other sites that were added to this list on 1 July 2004 were:
  - o **Denmark:** Greenland's Ilulissat Icefjord (40 240 ha). The sea mouth of Sermeq Kujalleq, one of the few glaciers through which the Greenland ice cap reaches the sea.

o **Indonesia:** Tropical Rainforest Heritage of Sumatra (2,5 million ha). This site includes three national parks: Gunung Leuser National Park, Kerinci Seblat National Park and Bukit Barisan Selatan National Park.

o **Russian Federation:** Natural System of Wrangel Island Reserve. The site is located above the Arctic Circle, and includes the mountainous Wrangel Island (7 608 km²), Herald Island (11 km²) and the surrounding waters.

o **Saint Lucia:** Pitons Management Area (2 909 ha). This site is near the town of Soufriere, and includes the Pitons – two volcanic spires (770 m and 743 m) that rise from the sea.

THE CAPE FLORAL REGION

- On 1 July 2004 the World Heritage Committee recognised the Cape Floral Region Protected Areas as South Africa's sixth World Heritage Site.
- The Cape Floral Region Protected Areas is a serial site, covering an area of more than 553 000 ha, and includes eight separate protected areas. It stretches in a crescent-shaped band from Nieuwoudtville in the north to Cape Town in the south, and then east to Grahamstown.
- The eight core protected areas in the Cape Floral Region Protected Areas are:
  - Table Mountain
  - De Hoop Nature Reserve
  - Boland mountain complex
  - Groot Winterhoek wilderness area
  - Swartberg mountains
  - Boosmansbos wilderness area
  - Cederberg wilderness area
  - Baviaanskloof
- The Cape Floral Kingdom is the smallest and the richest floral kingdom, and has the highest known concentration of plant species: 1 300 per 10 000 km². (The concentration in the South American rainforest, second on this list, is 400 per 10 000 km²).
- The Kirstenbosch National Botanical Garden also forms part of this site. No other natural World Heritage Site includes a botanical garden.
- It is one of the richest areas for plants in the world, and although it represents less than 0,5% of Africa's total land area, it is home to nearly 20% of the continent's flora. Most of its ecological and biological processes are associated with fynbos vegetation, which is unique to this region.

- The number of species per genus in the region (9:1) and the number of species per family (52) are among the highest for various species-rich regions in the world.
- At least 70% of the 9 600 plant species of the Cape Floral Kingdom are found nowhere else on Earth.
- The species density in the Cape Floral Region is also among the highest in the world, and displays the highest levels of endemism (31,9%).
- Fynbos contains more than a 5% cover of Cape reeds, as well as proteas, ericas and seven plant families found nowhere else in the world. The word 'fynbos' derives from a Dutch word for plants with fine leaves.
- Of the more than 7 700 fynbos plant species, 70% are endemic to the area. There are more than 600 different species of ericas (heaths) in this area – and only 26 species in the rest of the world.
- A remarkable feature of fynbos is the number of species that are found in small areas. The total world range of some species can grow on an area smaller than half a rugby field!
- The Cape Peninsula, including Table Mountain, has an area of only 470 km^2 (as big as London), but it is home to 2 285 different plant species. There are more plant species in this small area than in the whole of Great Britain, which is 5 000 times bigger. Table Mountain alone (57 km^2) supports 1 470 species.
- The Cape Flats has the world's highest concentration of endangered species in the world – a total of 15 species per km^2 are in danger of extinction. This area of 1 874 km^2 houses more than 1 466 species (of which 76 are found only here).
- About 75% of South Africa's rare and threatened plants are found in the fynbos biome.

SOUTH AFRICA'S NATIONAL BOTANICAL GARDENS

South Africa has eight national botanical gardens, which are situated all over the country, to introduce visitors to the rich variety of the country's plant life.

	Name	City/Town	Description
1	Free State NBG	Bloemfontein	400 plant species, 124 bird species, 54 reptile species and almost 50 mammal species.
2	Karoo Desert NBG	Worcester	400 Namaqualand flowers, 300 endangered species, 70 bird species. The only truly succulent garden in the southern hemisphere and in Africa.
3	Harold Porter NBG	Near Betty's Bay	Main fynbos species, 88 bird species.
4	Kirstenbosch NBG	Cape Town	Main fynbos species, natural forest; variety of South African plants, fragrance garden, medicinal garden, protea garden, peninsula garden, Van Riebeeck's hedge.

	Name	City/Town	Description
5	Lowveld NBG	Nelspruit	600 plant species occurring naturally in this region, 2 000 additional species, 650 indigenous trees.
6	Natal NBG	Pietermaritzburg	Plants of the eastern grasslands, 120 bird species.
7	Pretoria NBG	Pretoria	Houses the National Herbarium, 600 species of flowering plants, spring flowers (Namaqualand daisies and mesems), wisteria avenue, aloe collection.
8	Walter Sisulu NBG	Roodepoort	Succulent rockery, cycad garden, wetland plants, water garden, 220 bird species, including a breeding pair of majestic Verreaux's eagles.

Did you know?

- Kirstenbosch, the most famous of South Africa's national botanical gardens, was founded in 1913 to preserve the country's unique flora – the first botanical garden in the world with this aim.
- The eight gardens cultivate only indigenous plants, trees and flowers.

--------------------------------- CAPE TOWN ---------------------------------

- Cape Town's first railway line was opened from Cape Town to Eerste River on 13 February 1862, and extended to Wellington in 1863.
- The Cape Peninsula has one of the world's six plant kingdoms, with a total of 2 285 plant species (the British Isles have only 1 492 plant species). The sea around the peninsula is also home to 660 of the 2 008 sea animals that live along the South African coast.
- Dr Chris Barnard performed the world's first heart transplant in Cape Town's Groote Schuur hospital on 3 December 1967.
- Cape Town's famous noonday gun dates from the time when a cannon was shot at noon as a time check, especially for ships. Later the Observatory took to shooting a pistol at noon to alert ships, and eventually a cannon was fired. The gun was moved to Signal Hill in 1902, where it has been telling Capetonians every day since then (except Sundays) when it is noon. Because sound takes three seconds to travel 1 km, people hearing the gun in Milnerton or Observatory should add 18 or 20 seconds to the time.
- In California, America, you will find a tiny village called Capetown, a farming area close to Petrolia, where oil was first discovered in the USA.

—————————— TABLE MOUNTAIN ——————————

- Table Mountain can be seen as far as 200 km out at sea.
- It is 1 086 m high, 3 km long, and covered by 1 470 species of indigenous flora.
- The highest point is Maclear's Beacon (1 086 m).
- The mountains flanking Table Mountain are known as Devil's Peak, Lion's Head and Signal Hill.
- Devil's Peak's name comes from the legendary smoking match between Van Hunks and the devil, which ended in Van Hunks giving the devil some gunpowder to smoke. Old Nick obliged, and disappeared in a puff of smoke. When Table Mountain's 'cloak' or 'tablecloth' (low white clouds) appears, people would say: 'Old Van Hunks and the devil are at it again!'
- Signal Hill's name refers to the fact that it was used for signalling, initially by fires, and later by firing a cannon. The cannon (the noonday gun) is still fired today.
- The mountains behind Table Mountain are known as the Twelve Apostles.

————— SOUTH AFRICA: HIGHEST MOUNTAIN —————
PEAK IN EACH PROVINCE

	Province	Peak	Height (m)	Range
1	KwaZulu-Natal	Mafadi	3 446	Drakensberg
2	Free State	Namahadi	3 275	Maluti mountains
3	Eastern Cape	KwaDuma	3 019	Drakensberg
4	Mpumalanga	Die Berg (The Mountain)	2 331	Steenkampsberg
5	Western Cape	Seweweekspoort	2 325	Swartberg
6	Northern Cape	Unnamed peak (8 km from Kompasberg)	2 156	Sneeuberg
7	Limpopo	Iron Crown	2 126	Wolkberg
8	Gauteng	Nooitgedacht	1 852	Nooitgedacht
9	North-West	Nooitgedacht (western end)	1 800	Nooitgedacht

Did you know?

- 'Beautiful little mountain' is the name of the highest point in southern Africa, the 3 482-m high Thabana Ntlenyana in Lesotho. The second highest peak in southern Africa is Makheka, also in Lesotho. It is 20 m lower, at 3 462 m.
- The average height of the Drakensberg is 3 200 m above sea level. The length of the entire mountain range is some 900 km, and approximately 2 100 caves and rock shelters have been discovered to date.

HIGHEST MOUNTAINS IN AFRICA

	Mountain	Highest Summit	Height (m)	Country
1	Mount Kilimanjaro	Kibo-Uhuru Peak	5 892	Tanzania
2	Mount Kenya	Nelion Peak	5 199	Kenya
3	Mawensi	Hans Meyer Peak	5 149	Tanzania
4	Mount Stanley	Margherita Peak	5 109	DRC/Uganda
5	Mount Speke	Vittorio Emanuele Peak	4 890	Uganda
6	Mount Baker	Edward Peak	4 844	Uganda
7	Mount Emin	Umberto Peak	4 798	DRC
8	Mount Gessi	Iolanda Peak	4 715	Uganda
9	Mount Luigi di Savoia	Sella Peak	4 627	Uganda
10	Ras Dashen Terara	Ancua (alternate name)	4 620	Ethiopia

Did you know?

- Mount Kilimanjaro, an extinct volcano in northern Tanzania, is the highest mountain in Africa, and peaks at 5 892 m.
- Kilimanjaro has two peaks. Kibo, previously believed to be 5 895 m high, was 'cut down to size' after more accurate global positioning system (GPS) satellite equipment revealed that its true height was 5 892 m. Mawensi, the other peak, is 5 149 m high. The highest point on Kibo, which is actually a large crater, is known as Uhuru.

WORLD MOUNTAINS

	Peak	Location	Height (m)
1	Mount Everest	Nepal	8 850
2	K2	Pakistan/China	8 611
3	Kangchenjunga	Nepal/India	8 586
4	Lhotse	Nepal	8 516
5	Makalu	Nepal	8 462
6	Cho Oyu	Nepal	8 201
7	Dhaulagiri	Nepal	8 167
8	Manaslu	Nepal	8 156
9	Nanga Parbat	Pakistan	8 125
10	Annapurna	Nepal	8 091

Did you know?

- Everest is *not* the world's tallest mountain. This honour actually belongs to Mauna Kea, a volcanic mountain on Hawaii. It has a total height of 10 203 m, of which only 4 205 m is above sea level. Mauna Kea is about 1 353 m higher than Mount Everest, which is the highest mountain peak on land.

- Mount Everest was originally named 'Peak XV' when it was measured in the great trigonometrical survey of India. Its height was initially given as 8 839 m, according to a report in *The Times* of 4 October 1856. An Indian government survey in 1954 adapted this height to 8 848 m, but this was raised by 2 m to 8 850 m when the most modern GPS satellite equipment was used in 1999.

- Sir Andrew Waugh, surveyor-general of India, renamed Peak XV to Everest in 1856 to honour Sir George Everest, his predecessor. The local population have their own names for this giant. The Tibetans call it 'Chomo Lungma' (or Chomolangma/Chomolungma), which means 'goddess-mother', and the Nepalese name is 'Sagarmatha', meaning 'forehead in the sky'.

- Sir Edmund Hillary, a New Zealand beekeeper, and Nepal's Sherpa Tenzing Norgay, became the first people to reach the summit of Everest, on 29 May 1953.

- Mount Everest is 19,8 times higher than the Empire State Building in New York, and its height increases by about 4 mm per year.

- The first South African to climb Mount Everest was Cathy O'Dowd, who reached the 'top of the world' on 23 April 1996. Sibusiso Vilane and Sean Wisedale followed her, both in 2003.

- Sibusiso Vilane, a South African game ranger who was born in Swaziland, became the first black African to reach the top of Mount Everest. He achieved this feat a few days before the 50th anniversary of the first ascent by Edmund Hillary and Sherpa Tenzing Norgay.

- The world's second highest mountain is also in the Himalayas. It is known as K2 (because it was the second mountain in Kashmir's Karakoram range to be surveyed). The local people know it as Chogori or Dapsang, and it was previously called Mount Godwin Austen.

- The highest mountain range is in the Pacific Ocean. Its peaks can be seen on the islands of Hawaii.

- Australia is the continent with the lowest highest mountain. Mount Kosciuszko is only 2 228 m high.

- The highest mountain in the solar system is Olympus Mons, a volcanic mountain on Mars. It is higher than 25 000 m – nearly 3 times as high as Mount Everest.

THE HIGHEST MOUNTAINS ON THE SEVEN CONTINENTS

Mountain	Height (m)	Country	Continent
Aconcagua	6 962	Argentina	South America
Puncak Jaya (Carstensz Pyramid)	4 884	Indonesia	Oceania
Elbrus	5 633	Russia	Europe
Everest	8 850	Nepal/Tibet	Asia
Kilimanjaro	5 963	Tanzania	Africa
Mount Kosciuszko*	2 228	Australia	Australia
Mt McKinley	6 195	Alaska	North America
Vinson Massif	4 897	(Ellsworth Range)	Antarctica

* Eight mountains are listed, because some climbers feel that Mount Kosciuszko, which is the highest mountain on Australia, should be included, while others feel that Australia should be considered part of Oceania, which would mean that Puncak Jaya in Indonesia is included ...

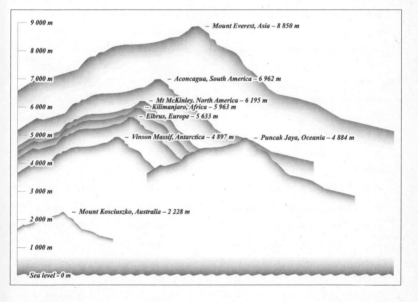

Did you know?
- The first South African and African to climb the highest mountain on each of the seven continents was film producer Sean Wisedale. He chose to climb Puncak Jaya and not Kosciuszko, and completed his climb in February 2004.
- Wisedale reached the top of Mount Vinson in Antarctica in 1998, Aconcagua (South America) in 2001, and Mount McKinley (North America) in 2002. In

2003, within the space of three months, he conquered three more mountains – Mount Everest (Asia) in May, Mount Elbrus (Europe) in August, and Puncak Jaya (Oceania).

- After his climb, Wisedale said: 'To be the first South African to have climbed all seven would be absolutely amazing ... The odds of reaching the summit of any mountain are not in favour of the climber, and so to reach the summit of the highest on each continent would be a gift from God.'
- By the beginning of May 2004, a total of 81 mountaineers had succeeded in climbing the Puncak Jaya version of the Seven Summits, and 87 had completed the Kosciuszko version. Because the two lists overlap to some extent, a total of only 123 climbers (not including Wisedale) have climbed the Seven Summits, with 46 of them having climbed all eight.
- The first two climbers to complete the Seven Summits were the American Dick Bass, on 30 April 1985, and Canada's Pat Morrow (Puncak Jaya), on 8 May 1986.
- Rob Hall and Gary Ball (both from New Zealand) completed the Seven Summits, with Kosciuszko, in six hours less than seven months. Britain's Andrew Salter completed the Seven Summits, with Puncak Jaya, in 297 days.

More mountain facts ...
- The patron saint of mountaineers is St Bernard of Menthon.
- The St Bernard, a large mountain dog that is sometimes used for rescue operations in the mountains, was named after this saint, who provided way stations for people who travelled in the Alps.

—— THE UKHAHLAMBA-DRAKENSBERG PARK ——

- The uKhahlamba-Drakensberg Park was the first South African site to be nominated as a mixed site (natural and cultural), and became the 23rd mixed site worldwide to achieve World Heritage Site status.
- About 6 000 sites and 35 000 individual rock paintings have been catalogued in the Drakensberg area. The oldest painting dates back about 2 400 years, but paint chips that are at least a thousand years older have also been found.
- San artists mixed natural materials such as clay, burnt wood and ochre oxides to get the predominant red, orange, yellow, black and white colours that they used.
- The park also has 2 153 plant species, of which 98 are endemic or near-endemic to this protected area, including the very rare *Protea nubigena*, which is found only on a high ridge in the Royal Natal sector.

• There are 299 recorded bird species in the uKhahlamba-Drakensberg Park and World Heritage Site – which is about 37% of South Africa's non-marine birds – as well as 48 species of mammals.

THE WORLD'S TALLEST BUILDINGS

No.	Building	City/Country	Year	Stories	Height (m)
1	Taipei 101 Tower	Taipei, Taiwan	2004	101	508
2	Petronas Tower 1	Kuala Lumpur, Malaysia	1998	88	452
3	Petronas Twin Tower 2	Kuala Lumpur, Malaysia	1998	88	452
4	Sears Tower	Chicago, USA	1974	110	442
5	Jin Mao Building	Shanghai, China	1999	88	421
6	Two International Finance Centre (IFC)	Hong Kong, China	2003	88	415
7	Sky Central Plaza (CITI Plaza, China International Trust)	Guanshou, China	1997	80	391
8	Shun Hing Square	Shenzhen, China	1996	69	384
9	Empire State Building	New York, USA	1931	102	381
10	Bank of China Tower	Hong Kong, China	1990	72	367

Forthcoming attractions ...

Building	City	By (date)	Floors	Height (m)
Centre of India Tower (speculative)	Katangi, India	2008 (projected)	224	677
Kowloon Station Phase 7 (MTR Tower)	Union Plaza, Hong Kong	2007 (projected)	102	574
Freedom Tower	New York City	Unknown	110	575

'Skyscraper (building), very tall, slender multi-storey building that, typically, and either singly or in groups, dominates the urban skyline, and towers above other buildings. Skyscrapers differ structurally from other buildings: whereas conventional buildings have load-bearing walls, skyscrapers consist of an iron or steel frame, to which non-load-bearing (and therefore thin, light) walls are attached.'

– *Encarta World Encyclopedia (2004)*

──── HIGH-RISE BUILDINGS IN SOUTH AFRICA ────

The Carlton Centre (50 stories) is the tallest office block in Africa, and the Hillbrow Tower (90 stories and 270 m) is the tallest tower. According to the Emporis Database of High-rise Buildings, Durban has the most high-rise buildings (174), followed by Cape Town (157) and Johannesburg (129).

	City	Buildings
1	Durban	174
2	Cape Town	157
3	Johannesburg	129
4	Port Elizabeth	19
5	Pretoria	15
6	Umhlanga Rocks	15
7	Amanzimtoti	12
8	Strand	12
9	Bellville	9
10	Bloemfontein	7

Durban (174 high-rise buildings)

	Name	Height (m)
1	88 on Field	147
2	Monte Blanc	133
3	Old Mutual Centre	131
4	Embassy Building	120
5	Holiday Inn Garden Court Marine Parade	118

Cape Town (157 high-rise buildings)

	Name	Height (m)
1	Metlife Centre	150
2	BP Centre	127
3	Shell House	119
4	ABSA Centre Cape Town	117
5	Golden Acre	108

Johannesburg (129 high-rise buildings)

	Name	Height (m)
1	Hillbrow Tower	270
2	Sentech Tower	234
3	Carlton Centre Office Tower	223
4	Ponte City Apartments	173
5	Kwa Dukuza Egoli Hotel	140

Port Elizabeth (19 high-rise buildings)

	Name	Floors
1	Sanport 140	22
2	University of Port Elizabeth Main Building	21
3	The Beaches	20
4	Post Office Port Elizabeth	19
5	Brister House	18

Pretoria (15 high-rise buildings)

	Name	Height (m)
1	John Vorster Tower	198
2	South African Reserve Bank	150
3	ABSA Building	132
4	Poyntons Building	110
5	Agricultural Union Centre	110

Bloemfontein (seven high-rise buildings)

	Building name (Project name)	Floors
1	Loch Logan Park	27
2	Free State Provincial Government Building I	26
3	Free State Provincial Government Building II	13
4	Universitas Private Hospital	13
5	Chester Hill	13

The Carlton Centre

- The Carlton Centre Office Tower has an observation deck on the 50th floor, which gives a bird's eye view of the city of Johannesburg.
- The Carlton Centre was sold in 1999 for R33 million and houses the head office of Transnet.
- The Carlton Centre was the tallest building in the southern hemisphere when completed, and is still the tallest building in Africa.
- It houses the largest parking arcade of any city in South Africa.

JOHANNESBURG

- Johannesburg was founded on 4 October 1886, making it one of the world's youngest major cities.
- The first tent, belonging to J Paxton de Roi, was erected on 9 July 1886, more than two months before President Paul Kruger declared the area open for public digging on 20 September 1886. It was initially a tent town, but wooden and iron shacks replaced the tents, with brick buildings following within a few years, and Johannesburg became a city in 1928. Today it has a population of 3,2 million.
- Johannesburg is 1 763 m above sea level. That is why the air is thinner, and it takes a minute longer to boil an egg than in Cape Town or Durban.
- Johannesburg has quite a number of nicknames: Jozi, Egoli (which means 'Place of Gold') and City of Gold.
- Johannesburg has 6 million trees (1,2 million in parks and on pavements, and 4,8 million at private homes).
- The 9 247 km of roads (of which only 1 040 km is not tarred) are illuminated by 180 000 streetlights, and the traffic is regulated by 1 780 traffic lights. The 554 buses operate on 80 routes and transport about 20 million passengers every year.
- Johannesburg is quite a common name. There is a Johannesburg in Suriname, and in California, Wisconsin and Michigan in the USA.

SOUTH AFRICA'S MINERAL WEALTH

Mineral	Reserves (ton)	Percentage of world total	World ranking
Gold	40 000	39	1
Chromium (ore)	3,1 billion	68	1
Alumino-silicates	50,8 million	37	1
Manganese ore	4 billion	80	1
Platinum group metals	62 800	56	1
Titanium minerals	146 million	31	1
Vanadium	12,5 million	45	1
Vermiculite	80 million	40	2
Zirconium minerals	14,3 million	23	2
Fluorspar	36 million	10	3
Phosphates	0,5 million	8	3
Antimony	250 000	5	4
Coal	55 billion	11	5
Diamonds	–	–	5
Lead	3 million	2	5
Uranium	204 000	7	5
Zinc	15 million	4	5
Iron ore	5,9 billion	6	8
Copper	13 million	2	13

——— GOLD ———

Properties and measurements of Aurum

Chemical symbol	Au
Latin name	Aurum
Meaning	Glowing dawn
Origin of word	From an Indo-European root, meaning 'yellow'
Melting point	1 064 °C
Boiling point	2 808 °C
Largest gold reserves	USA
	Germany
	International Monetary Fund (IMF)
Most gold produced per year	South Africa (500 tons)
	USA (320 tons)
Annual production (2001)	2 604 tons (67% of the total demand)
Total of all gold mined	145 000 tons (if all the gold ever produced is made into a thin wire with a diameter of 5 microns (1 micron = 1 millionth of a metre), it would stretch 72 million times around the Earth.
Gold is weighed in	Troy ounce (31,103475 grams)

Troy ounces in a ton	32 151
Density of gold	19,32 g/cm³
Volume of 1 troy ounce	1,64 cm³
Volume of 1 ton	51 760 cm³ (a cube with sides of 37,27 cm)
Largest gold refinery	Rand Refinery (South Africa). It has refined over 40 000 tons (1 286 million ounces) in its history – about 30% of all gold ever mined. The refinery opened in 1921 to refine South Africa's gold, which was previously refined in London. It was rebuilt in the late 1980s.

GOLD PRICE 1900–2004

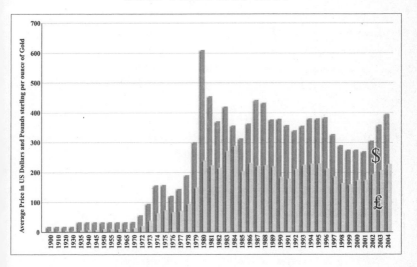

Did you know?

- The USA holds the world's largest gold reserves at Fort Knox, near Louisville, Kentucky. The gold (more than 147 million fine ounces, or 8 136,4 tons) is kept in bomb-proof safes, and is protected by armed guards.
- Germany (with 3 439,5 tons) is second on the list, followed by the IMF (3 217,3 tons) and France (3 024,6 tons).
- George Harrison, who discovered South Africa's wealth in gold in 1886, sold his claim for £10.
- All the gold ever mined in the world would fit into a room measuring 17 m long, 17 m high and 17 m wide (approximately 5 000 m³).
- More steel is poured in an hour than all the gold that has been poured since the

beginning of time.
- The world's dentists use over 60 tons of gold every year.
- At least 15% of the annual gold consumption is recycled each year.
- The largest gold nugget ever discovered was called Welcome Stranger, and weighed 70,92 kg. It was discovered in 1869 in the state of Victoria, Australia – in a cartwheel rut – and contained 69,92 kg of pure gold.
- The largest single mass of gold was the Holtermann nugget (a mixture of gold and quartz), which weighed 235,14 kg, and was found in 1872 in New South Wales, Australia. It contained 82,11 kg of pure gold.
- There is gold in seawater – approximately 0,004 mg per ton – but getting it out of the sea is the problem. The US Dow Chemical Company in North Carolina laboriously processed 15 tons of seawater, and only succeeded in collecting 0,09 mg of gold, which was worth about a hundredth of a US cent.
- The world's largest golden statue is the 15th-century Sukhotai Traimit statue of Buddha in Bangkok, Thailand. It is 5,4 m high and weighs 5,4 tons.
- The gold price reached its highest level on 21 January 1980, when one ounce was worth $850.
- A gold ingot as big as a matchbox can be beaten so thin that it can cover a tennis court. This gold will have a thickness of 0,00001 mm.
- Monuments and coffins in ancient Egypt were often plated with gold, which was hand-beaten to a thickness of 0,0002 mm.

∽ HOW BIG IS A GOLD BAR? ∽

Weight	Length	Width	Depth
400 oz	200 mm	80 mm	45 mm
1 kg	80 mm	40 mm	18 mm
500 g	65 mm	32 mm	14 mm
250 g	55 mm	25 mm	10 mm
100 g	55 mm	31 mm	3 mm
50 g	45 mm	25 mm	2,3 mm
1 oz	42 mm	24 mm	2 mm
20 g	39 mm	22 mm	1,3 mm
10 g	31 mm	18 mm	1 mm
5 g	23 mm	14 mm	0,7 mm
1 g	15 mm	8 mm	0,4 mm

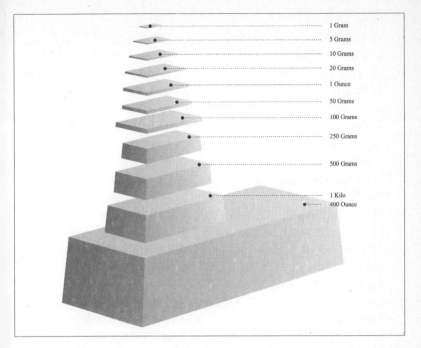

PRETORIA

- Pretoria is known as the Jacaranda City, because of the multitude of jacaranda trees that decorate the city's streets with their mauve flowers in spring. Jacaranda flowers are usually mauve, but they can also be white.

- Pretoria's main street, Church Street, is the longest urban street in South Africa. It measures 26 km from end to end.

- Anton van Wouw's statue of Paul Kruger first stood in front of Princes Park, and later in front of the Pretoria Station, but was moved to Church Square, where it was unveiled on 10 October 1954.

- The Cullinan was the largest of all known rough diamonds ever found. It weighed 3 106 carats (or 621,2 g), and was named after Sir Thomas Cullinan, the owner of the Premier diamond mine, near Pretoria, where it was found. It was cut into three large parts in Amsterdam, and the largest polished gem was called Cullinan I, or the Great Star of Africa. It weighs 530,2 carats, and is the largest polished diamond in the world. It is mounted in the head of the British royal sceptre. The second largest gem, known as Cullinan II (or the Lesser Star of Africa) weighs 317,4 carats and forms part of the British crown.

THE VOORTREKKER MONUMENT

- Pretoria's impressive Voortrekker Monument was built in honour of the Voortrekkers, who left the Cape Colony between 1835 and 1854. The architect was Gerard Moerdijk.

- The first plans to build a monument in honour of the Voortrekkers were made as early as 16 December 1895, when General Piet Joubert laid the foundation stone of the memorial at Bloukrans, near Chievely, Natal. A committee was formed there and then to collect funds, but as no real progress was made, the committee ceased to exist.

- The Sentrale Volksmonumentekomitee (SVK, or Central National Monuments Committee) was only formed in 1931 to plan the monument.

- The final site for the Voortrekker Monument, Monument Hill, just outside Pretoria, was selected in 1936.

- Advocate EG Jansen, chairman of the SVK, turned the first sod on 13 July 1937, and Mrs JC Muller, a granddaughter of Andries Pretorius, Mrs KF Ackerman, a great-granddaughter of Hendrik Potgieter, and Mrs JC Preller, a great-granddaughter of Piet Retief, laid the cornerstone on 16 December 1938. The construction was stopped by the outbreak of the Second World War.

- In 1940, when new tenders for the construction of the monument were invited, an offer by WF du Plessis was accepted. He used stone from granite quarries near Zoutpansberg, and completed the monument in 1949.

- Dr DF Malan inaugurated the monument on 16 December 1949 with his famous '*Quo Vadis*, South Africa?' speech.

Visiting the Voortrekker Monument
- Visitors to the Voortrekker Monument enter the complex through a black wrought-iron gate with an assegai motif, which symbolises Dingaan's power.

- Inside the gate they will see a large wagon laager, which symbolically protects the monument. The laager wall has 64 wagons – the number of wagons drawn into a laager at Blood River on 16 December 1838.

- A bronze sculpture of a Voortrekker mother and her two children, created by Anton van Wouw, stands at the entrance to the monument. This was his last major work.

- On both sides of this sculpture are black wildebeest, which are chiselled into the walls of the monument.

- The foundation stone is on the eastern corner, on the same level as the entrance to the monument.
- The four figures depicted at the four corners of the monument are Piet Retief, Andries Pretorius, Hendrik Potgieter and an unknown leader (who represents all the other Voortrekker leaders). Each of these figures weighs about 6 tons.

Inside the monument ...
- Beyond the Voortrekker Monument's massive teak front doors is the Hall of Heroes.
- It is a huge domed hall ($25 \times 25 \times 41$ m), with marble floors and a marble frieze, which depicts historical scenes from the Great Trek.
- The frieze that lines the walls ...
    - consists of 27 marble panels
    - is 2,3 m high
    - extends for 92 m
    - weighs about 200 tons.
- The frieze, which depicts the main events of the Great Trek, was designed by the South African sculptors Hennie Potgieter, Peter Kirchhoff, Frikkie Kruger and Laurika Postma, and sculpted from Italian Quercetta marble by 40 Italian chisellers and six Italian sculptors.
- The total cost for the construction of the frieze was £60 000.
- Each of the four huge arched windows in the Hall of Heroes consists of 1 072 pieces of yellow Belgian glass.
- The floor of the Hall of Heroes was made from marble excavated from the marble quarries near Marble Hall.
- The floor forms a pattern, which looks like water rippling out in widening circles, with the cenotaph in the middle. This is symbolical of the trek to freedom, which began on a small scale, but later became a migratory flood in South African history.

The cenotaph
- The cenotaph is the central focus point of the monument, and one can see it and the interior of the monument from an arch at the top of the Hall of Heroes.
- At twelve o'clock on 16 December every year, the sun shines precisely on the middle of the cenotaph, illuminating the words '*Ons vir jou Suid-Afrika*' ['We for thee, South Africa']. The cenotaph represents the symbolic resting place of Piet Retief and all the Voortrekkers who died during the Great Trek.

- The cenotaph was made of red granite from Parys in the Orange Free State.
- The nave in the Cenotaph Hall contains a flame that has been kept burning since the 1938 Symbolic Ox-wagon Trek.

Did you know?
- The Voortrekker Monument is 62 m high.
- There are:
  - 130 steps from the parking lot to the main entrance of the Voortrekker Monument
  - 169 steps from the Hall of Heroes to the top of the building
  - 38 steps from the Hall of Heroes down to the Cenotaph Hall.
- The items that were placed behind the cornerstone when it was laid are:
  - A copy of Jan van Riebeeck's diary
  - A copy of the Piet Retief–Dingaan Treaty
  - A copy of the vow of 16 December 1838
  - A copy of 'The Call of South Africa'
  - Mr Henning Klopper's family Bible.
- The total cost for the construction of the Voortrekker Monument was £359 600.

SOUTH AFRICA'S LARGEST MUNICIPAL AREAS

	Metropolitan area	Description	Population	
1	Buffalo City	East London	701 890	**Buffalo City** is centred around East London and King William's Town.
2	Cape Town	Cape Town	2 893 246	The **City of Cape Town** was founded on 6 December 2000, and consists of the seven former local metropolitan councils: Blaauwberg Municipality, City of Cape Town, City of Tygerberg, Helderberg Municipality, Oostenberg Municipality, South Peninsula Municipality and the Cape Metropolitan Council.
3	Ekurhuleni Metro	East Rand	2 480 277	The **Ekurhuleni** Municipality consists of nine towns of the former East Rand – Greater Alberton, Benoni, Germiston, Springs, Kempton Park, Edenvale, Nigel, Brakpan and Boksburg. *Ekurhuleni* is a Xitsonga word, which means 'the place of peace'.

	Metropolitan area	Description	Population	
4	eThekwini	Durban	3 090 121	**eThekwini** includes seven council areas and some tribal land, and stretches from Umkomaas in the south, including some tribal area in Umbumbulu, to Tongaat in the north, with a tribal area in Ndwedwe. It ends at Cato Ridge in the west. *eThekwini* refers to Durban Bay, and means 'at the Bay'.
5	Mangaung Municipality	Bloemfontein	645 441	The **Mangaung** Municipality includes Bloemfontein and two other towns, Botshabelo and Thaba Nchu, and a rural area. *Mangaung* means 'place of the cheetahs'.
6	Nelson Mandela	Port Elizabeth	1 005 778	The **Nelson Mandela** Metropolitan Municipality incorporated Port Elizabeth, with its neighbouring towns of Uitenhage and Despatch, as well as the surrounding areas, in 2001.
7	Tshwane	Pretoria	1 985 983	**Tshwane** consists of the Greater Pretoria Metropolitan Council, City Council of Pretoria, Centurion, Akasia, Hammanskraal, Eastern District Council, Eastern Gauteng Services Council, Western Gauteng Services Council, Pienaarsrivier, Crocodile River, Winterveld, Themba, Mabopane and Ga-Rankuwa.
8	Msunduzi	Pietermaritzburg	553 223	**Msunduzi** is situated around Pietermaritzburg and surrounding areas. *Msunduzi* probably means 'push aside' or 'move', referring to the floodwaters pushing everything out of its way.
9	Johannesburg	Johannesburg	3 225 812	The **Johannesburg** Metropolitan area includes Sandton, Randburg, Roodepoort and Soweto.

CITY NICKNAMES

City	Nicknames					
Pretoria	Jacaranda City	Snor City				
Johannesburg	Egoli	Jozi	Joeys	Jo'burg	City of Gold	Goudstad
Port Elizabeth	PE	The Windy City	The Friendly City	The Bay	Die Baai	iBayi
Cape Town	The Mother City	iKapa	The Cape			
Bloemfontein	City of Roses	Die Rosestad	Mangaung			
Pietermaritzburg	uMgungundlovu					
Durban	eThekwini	Durbs				

---------------------------------- DURBAN ----------------------------------

- Durban was named after Sir Benjamin D'Urban, governor of the Cape Colony. It was originally named Rio de Natal and Port Natal, because Vasco da Gama arrived here on Chistmas Day in 1497. The 'Natal' refers to the birth of Christ.
- The Natal Railway opened the first railway in South Africa, which ran the 3 km from Durban to The Point, on 26 June 1860.
- The first electric rail operation in South Africa was used in Durban in 1926.

-------------------------- PREVIOUSLY KNOWN AS ... --------------------------

South Africa's cities and towns have some very interesting names, which mirror the rich variety of people and cultures in this country. Many of these cities and towns are not known by their original names any more, and some have even been renamed three or four times. Here are a number of these name changes. Some names were changed after the place had been well established as a city or town; others changed names almost immediately, forsaking the name of the original farm, village or hamlet for a more acceptable and appropriate name.

Town/City	Founded	Previous name(s)	Province
Heidelberg	1866	Langlaagte*	Gauteng
Johannesburg	1886	Randjeslaagte*	Gauteng
Krugersdorp	1887	Paardekraal*	Gauteng
Pretoria	1855	Elandspoort*; Pretoria Philadelphia; Pretorium; Pretoriusdorp	Gauteng
Soweto	1905	Doornkop*; Klipriviersoog*; Diepkloof*; Klipspruit* and Vogelstruisfontein*	Gauteng
Vereeniging	1882	Klipplaatsdrift* and Leeuwkuil*	Gauteng
Durban	1835	Rio de Natal; Port Natal	KwaZulu-Natal
Ladysmith	1850	Windsor; Juanasburg	KwaZulu-Natal
Jan Kempdorp	1953	Andalusia	Northern Cape
Kimberley	1873	Colesberg Kopje; De Beer's New Rush; Vooruitzicht	Northern Cape
Upington	1871	Oljvenhoutsdrift	Northern Cape
Bela-Bela	1882	Het Bad*; Noodshulp*; Roodepoort*; Turfbult*, Badplaas; Hartingsburg; Warmbaths	Limpopo
Makhoda	1899	Bergvliet* and Rietvlei*; Louis Trichardt	Limpopo
Modimole	1866	Rietvlei*; Nylstroom	Limpopo
Mokopane	1852	Vredenburg; Pietpotgietersrust; Potgietersrust; Potgietersrus	Limpopo
Musina	1904	Berkenrode*; Messina	Limpopo
Polokwane	1884	Sterkloop*; Pietersburg	Limpopo
Zeerust	1867	Sebatlani*; Hazenjacht*; Coetzee-Rust	North West
East London	1845	Port Rex	Eastern Cape
Port Elizabeth	1799	Fort Frederick	Eastern Cape

Town/City	Founded	Previous name(s)	Province
Somerset East	1825	Boschberg	Eastern Cape
Bethulie	1863	Heidelberg	Free State
Bellville	1861	Twelve Mile Stone	Western Cape
Bredasdorp	1838	Lange Fontein	Western Cape
Caledon	1715	Zwarte Berg; Zwartbergbad; 't Warme Bad	Western Cape
Cape Town	1652	Cabo de Goede Hoop; De Caab; Het Vlek van de Caab	Western Cape
Darling	1853	Groene Kloof	Western Cape
Durbanville	1806	Pampoenkraal; D'Urban	Western Cape
Franschhoek	1860	Olifantshoek	Western Cape
Ladismith	1852	Elandsvlei; Lady Smith	Western Cape
Malmesbury	1829	Swartland	Western Cape
Mossel Bay	1848	Aguado de Sâo Bras; Golfo dos Vaqueiros; Aliwal-Suid	Western Cape
Oudtshoorn	1847	Hartebeestrivier	Western Cape
Strand	1850	Van Ryneveld's Town; Hottentots-Holland Strand; Somerset Strand; The Strand	Western Cape
Vredenburg	1883	Procesfontein	Western Cape
Wellington	1840	Wagenmakers Valley	Western Cape
Worcester	1820	Langerug* and Roodewal*; Boschjesveld	Western Cape

* Indicates the name of the original farm on which the town was established.

MONOPOLY

In 1934 Charles B Darrow of Germantown, Pennsylvania, presented a boardgame called 'The Monopoly Game' to the Parker Brothers executives. They rejected it because of design errors (52 of them!). Mr Darrow, who was unemployed, produced the game on his own, and sold 5 000 to a department store in Philadelphia. When he couldn't keep up with the demand, he went back to Parker Brothers.

Since 1935, more than 200 million copies have been sold worldwide, and more than 500 million people have played the classic game. Monopoly is sold in 80 countries and has been translated into 26 languages. More than 5 billion of the famous little green houses have been built since then.

In 1999, Hasbro Inc. introduced a new token for the game of Monopoly – a sack of money. It was the first addition in more than 40 years, and it was chosen over the piggy bank and the biplane in a big public campaign. The voters also named the racing car as their favourite existing token.

With the addition of the sack of money, there are now 11 tokens included in the classic Monopoly game. The last new tokens added to the Monopoly game (the dog, wheelbarrow, and horse and rider) were introduced in the early 1950s.

The 11 tokens used internationally are: sack of money, battleship, cannon, dog, horse and rider, iron, racing car, shoe, thimble, top hat and wheelbarrow.

The first Monopoly games were probably introduced to South Africa in 1963, and were produced by Metrotoy under licence of John Waddington Ltd. Production was later taken over by Prima Toys, which introduced new properties in 2002.

Monopoly in South Africa: old game (1963–2002)				
Durban	**Bloemfontein**	**Cape Town**	**Johannesburg**	**Stations**
Brown	*Pink*	*Red*	*Green*	Durban
Musgrave Rd	Monument Rd	Groote Schuur St	Main St	Bloemfontein
Gillespie St	Aliwal St	Strand St	Joubert St	Cape Town
	Maitland St	Roeland St	De Villiers St	Johannesburg
Blue	*Orange*	*Yellow*	*Purple*	
West St	President Brand St	Parliament St	Jan Smuts Ave	
Smith St	Hoffmann Sq	Plain St	Eloff St	
Marine Parade	Voortrekker Sq	Long St		

Monopoly in South Africa: new game (since 2002)					
KwaZulu-Natal	**Johannesburg**	**Western Cape**	**Eastern Cape**	**Pretoria**	**Garden Route**
Brown	*Red*	*Green*	*Pink*	*Pink*	*Orange*
Westville	Hillbrow	Mitchells Plain	Port Elizabeth	Menlyn Park	Wilderness
Amanzimtoti	Soweto	Tygervalley		Waterkloof	Knysna
	Boksburg	Bloubergstrand			Plettenberg Bay
Blue	*Yellow*	*Purple*	**Airports**		
Umhlanga Rocks	Randburg	Franschhoek	Durban International		
Ballito Bay	Sandton	Clifton	Johannesburg International		
La Lucia	Hyde Park		Bloemfontein International		
			Cape Town International		

Banknotes

The new South African game has seven different Monopoly banknotes, and the denominations are: R1, R5, R10, R20, R50, R100, R500.

The salary that players 'earn' when they pass BEGIN has gone up from R200 to R20 000.

Tokens

The six plastic tokens included in the game are: top hat, iron, shoe, racing car, battleship, dog.

─────────── PORT ELIZABETH ───────────

• Port Elizabeth was originally known as Fort Frederick, which is the name of the oldest stone building in the Eastern Cape and the earliest permanent structure still in existence.

- It was renamed Port Elizabeth in 1820, after Elizabeth Frances Donkin, the wife of Sir Rufane Donkin, the acting governor of the Cape Colony. She had died two years earlier in India.

Port Elizabeth has a number of firsts to its credit. It had …
- the first joint stock mining company in South Africa, known as the Maitland Mining Company (1846);
- the first diamond auction in South Africa (1869);
- the first overseas shipment of South African gold (1874);
- the first experimental wireless transmission in South Africa (1897);
- the first South African bowling association (1904);
- the first snake park in South Africa (1910);
- the first mail order business in South Africa (1910); and
- the first motor car and truck assembly plant (1924).

Did you know?
- The first cricket test in South Africa was played on 12 and 13 March 1889 at St George's Park in Port Elizabeth, against an English team brought to South Africa by Major R Gardner Warton, with Charles Aubrey Smith as captain. Smith's angled run-up led to his nickname 'Round the corner Smith'. OR Dunell captained South Africa.
- South Africa batted first and scored 84, to which England replied with 148. In their second innings, South Africa's score was 129, and England then scored 67 runs for the loss of only two wickets.
- The first woman's cricket test match in South Africa was also played in Port Elizabeth, in 1960.

CRICKET: BALLS PER OVER

A normal cricket over, without any no-balls or wides, will contain six balls. (If the umpire miscounts – and it does happen, even in tests – a 'normal' over can be abbreviated to five balls, or extended to seven balls.) The number of balls bowled per over has changed considerably over the past 130 years (see table below).

England	Balls	Australia	Balls	South Africa	Balls	New Zealand	Balls
1880–1888	4	1876/77–1887/88	4	1888/89	4	1929/30–1967/68	6
1890–1899	5	1891/92–1920/21	6	1891/92–1898/99	5	1968/69–1978/79	8
1902–1938	6	1924/25	8	1902/03–1935/36	6	1979/80–	6
1939	8	1928/29–1932/33	6	1938/39–1957/58	8		
1946–	6	1936/37–1978/79	8	1961/62–	6		
		1979/80–	6				

RUGBY UNION: SCORING CHANGES

The ultimate goal for any rugby team is to score tries – lots and lots of them. In the beginning, much, much more than a century ago, the *try* was called so because a player would 'try' for a goal after scoring a try. A *try* would count 1 point, and the conversion would treble that score. Gradually the try became more and more important, and took its rightful place in the scoring system.

Season	Try	Conversion	Penalty	Drop goal	Goal fr. mark
1891	1	2	2	3	3
1892–1893	2	3	3	4	4
1894–1905	3	2	3	4	4
1906–1947	3	2	3	4	3
1948–1971	3	2	3	3	3
1972–1977	4	2	3	3	3
1978–1992	4	2	3	3	–
1992–	5	2	3	3	–

Did you know?

- The first rugby test in South Africa was also played in Port Elizabeth. It took place on the PE Cricket Ground on Thursday 30 July 1891, against a British touring team led by WE Maclagan. HH Castens (who was the referee in the third test!) captained South Africa. The British Isles won the test 4-0 (two 1-point tries and a conversion).

- The first rugby test played by a South African women's team (or female Springboks) was played in Port Elizabeth on Saturday 29 May 2004. The women Boks lost 5-8 to Wales, and Ronwyn Kelly (wing) scored South Africa's first try ever in a test. The referee, Jenny Bentel (Western Province), was also the first South African woman to carry the whistle in a test.

- In the second test against Wales, played a week later at Loftus, Nadine Barnard and Ronwyn Kelly scored the tries, and Anne-Marie van Biljon succeeded with a conversion and a penalty. Wales clinched the victory, however, with a last-minute penalty. The final score was 16-15.

--------------------------------- BLOEMFONTEIN ---------------------------------

- Bloemfontein was probably named after flowers (Dutch 'bloemen') growing at the fountain, and was founded in 1846.
- Bloemfontein was the birthplace of the author John Ronald Reuel (JRR) Tolkien (1892–1973), who created the imaginary Middle Earth and the fictional language Elvish. His first novel was *The Hobbit* (1937), and he wrote its sequel, the trilogy *The Lord of the Rings*, between 1954 and 1955.
- South Africa's most influential political parties of the 20th century, the African National Congress and the National Party, were both founded in Bloemfontein – the ANC in 1912 and the NP in 1914.
- The city is also known as 'City of Roses', and King's Park has more than 4 000 rose bushes.
- The Franklin Game Reserve on Naval Hill is the only city centre game reserve in the world.

--------------------------------- VRYSTAAAAAT! ---------------------------------

That's what rugby lovers used to shout. Or even, '*Haak, Vrystaaaaat!*' ['Hook, Free State!']. The Free State was actually first known as Trans Orange – beyond the Orange (river).

The Orange River was not named for its colour – it honoured the Dutch House of Orange. The original Khoi name was Gariep, a name that was later given to the Hendrik Verwoerd Dam, South Africa's largest storage dam. The Orange River is also known as the Grootrivier (Big river/Great river).

Way back when South Africa was divided in four provinces, the Vrystaters (Free Staters) were nicknamed 'blikore' [tin ears]. People in the Cape Province were 'woltone' [woolly toes] and the Transvalers were 'vaalpense'. The Natalians were sometimes called 'piesangboere' [banana farmers].

--------------------------- THE ORIGINAL PROVINCES ---------------------------

Province	Area (km²)	Capital
Cape Province	716 653	Cape Town
Orange Free State	129 150	Bloemfontein
Natal	86 970	Pietermaritzburg
Transvaal	283 918	Pretoria

Did you know?

- In 1910, each of the four provincial capitals was also regarded as one of South Africa's capitals.
- Pretoria was the **administrative capital**, Cape Town the **legislative capital**, Bloemfontein the **judicial capital** and Pietermaritzburg the **archival capital**.

─────────── NAMES OF THE NINE PROVINCES ───────────

Current name	Original name(s)	Date of change
Northern Cape	Northern Cape	No change
Eastern Cape	Eastern Cape	No change
Free State	Orange Free State	29 June 1995
Western Cape	Western Cape	No change
Limpopo	Northern Transvaal	June 1995
	Northern Province	14 February 2002
North West	North West	No change
KwaZulu-Natal	KwaZulu-Natal	No change
Mpumalanga	Eastern Transvaal	25 August 1995
Gauteng	Pretoria–Witwatersrand–Vereeniging	8 December 1995

─────────── THE NINE PROVINCES – ───────────
FACTS AND FIGURES

Province	Capital	Area (km²)	% of SA	Population	% of population
Northern Cape	Kimberley	361 800	29,7	822 727	1,83
Eastern Cape	Bisho	169 600	13,9	6 436 763	14,34
Free State	Bloemfontein	129 480	10,6	2 706 775	6,17
Western Cape	Cape Town	129 370	10,6	4 524 335	10,08
Limpopo	Polokwane	123 280	10,2	5 273 642	11,75
North West	Mafikeng	116 190	9,5	3 669 349	8,18
KwaZulu-Natal	Pietermaritzburg Ulundi	92 180	7,6	9 426 017	21,00
Mpumalanga	Nelspruit	78 370	6,5	3 122 990	6,96
Gauteng	Johannesburg	18 810	1,4	8 837 178	19,69
RSA total	–	1 219 080			

PROVINCIAL TONGUES –
HOME LANGUAGES

Province	Language 1	Percentage	Language 2	Percentage	Language 3	Percentage
Northern Cape	Afrikaans	68,0	Setswana	20,8	IsiXhosa	6,2
Eastern Cape	IsiXhosa	83,4	Afrikaans	9,3	English	3,6
Free State	Sesotho	64,4	Afrikaans	11,9	IsiXhosa	9,1
Western Cape	Afrikaans	55,3	IsiXhosa	23,7	English	19,3
Limpopo	Sepedi	52,1	Xitsonga	22,4	Tshivenda	15,9
North West	Setswana	65,4	Afrikaans	7,5	IsiXhosa	5,8
KwaZulu-Natal	IsiZulu	80,9	English	13,6	Afrikaans	1,5
Mpumalanga	SiSwati	30,8	IsiZulu	26,4	IsiNdebele	12,1
Gauteng	IsiZulu	21,5	Afrikaans	14,4	Sesotho	13,1
					English	12,5

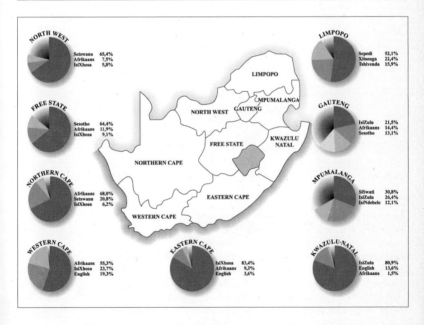

SOUTH AFRICA'S 11 OFFICIAL LANGUAGES

South Africa is the only country in the world with 11 official languages:

- Afrikaans
- IsiXhosa
- Sesotho
- Xitsonga
- English
- IsiNdebele
- Setswana
- Tshivenda
- IsiZulu
- Sepedi
- SiSwati

The official languages of the Union of South Africa, which was founded in 1910, were Dutch and English, and Afrikaans was added on 8 May 1925. Dutch was the third official language until 1961, when South Africa became a republic with only two official languages – Afrikaans and English.

Home language	Speakers	Home language	Speakers	Home language	Speakers
IsiZulu	10 677 305	IsiXhosa	7 907 153	Afrikaans	5 983 426
Sepedi	4 208 980	Setswana	3 677 016	Engels	3 673 203
Sesotho	3 555 186	Xitsonga	1 992 207	SiSwati	1 194 430
Tshivenda	1 021 757	IsiNdebele	711 821		

English	Afrikaans	Sesotho	Setswana	SiSwati	Tshivenda	Xitsonga
Expressions	Uitdrukkings	Ho i hlalosa	Tlhagiso-maikutlo	Tibingelelo	Kuambele	Tinhlamuselo
Good morning	Goeiemôre	Dumela	Dumela	Sawubona/ Kusile	Ndi matsheloni	Avuxeni
Goodbye	Tot siens	Sala hantle	Sala/Tsamaya sentle	Sala kahle/ Usale	Vha/Ni sale zwavhuḓi	Salani
Goodnight	Goeienag	Robala hantle	Robala sentle	Ulale kahle/ Unjani	Ndi made-kwana avhuḓi	Mi etlela kahle
How are you?	Hoe gaan dit?	O phetse jwang?	O kae?	Ngiyaphila/ Ngikhona?	No/Vho vuwa hani?	Ku njhani?
I am fine	Dit gaan goed	Ke petse	Ke teng	Ngiyacela	Ndo/Ro vuwa zwavhuḓi	Hi pfukile
Please	Asseblief	Ke kopa	Ka kopo	Ngiyabonga	Ndi khou tou humbela	Ndza kombela
Thank you	Dankie	Ke a leboha	Ke a leboga		Ndo livhuwa/ Ro livhuwa	Inkomu

English	IsiZulu	IsiXhosa	IsiNdebele	Sepedi
Expressions	Izimozo-kukhuluma	Amabinzana entetho	Ukuveza amazizo	Mebollelwana
Good morning	Sawubona	Molo	Lotjhani	Dumelang
Goodbye	Sala kahle	Sala kakuhle	Sala/Khamba kuhle	Salang gabotse
Goodnight	Lala kamnandi	Busuku benzolo	Ubusuku obumnandi	A ebe boroko
How are you?	Unjani?	Kunjani?	Kunjani?	Le/O kae?
I am fine	Ngiyaphila	Ndiphilile	Ngikhona	Ke gona
Please	Ngiyacela	Nceda	Ngiyabawa	Ka kgopelo
Thank you	Ngiyabonga	Enkosi	Ngiyathokoza	Ke a leboga

'SOUTH AFRICA' - IN 11 TONGUES

Republiek van Suid-Afrika (**Afrikaans**)
Republic of South Africa (**English**)
IRiphabliki yeSewula Afrika (**IsiNdebele**)
Rephaboliki ya Afrika-Borwa (**Sepedi**)
Rephaboliki ya Afrika Borwa (**Sesotho**)
IRiphabhulikhi yeNingizimu Afrika (**SiSwati**)
Riphabliki ra Afrika Dzonga (**Xitsonga**)
Rephaboliki ya Aforika Borwa (**Setswana**)
Riphabu'iki ya Afurika Tshipembe (**Tshivenda**)
IRiphabliki yaseMzantsi Afrika (**IsiXhosa**)
IRiphabliki yaseNingizimu Afrika (**IsiZulu**)

THE NATIONAL ANTHEM

- South Africa's national anthem consists of three different anthems, namely 'Nkosi Sikelel' iAfrika', 'Die Stem van Suid-Afrika' and 'The Call of South Africa', which are all blended into one song. The 'new' anthem uses five different languages, of which four are used at the same time (Xhosa or Zulu, together with Sesotho, Afrikaans and English).

- **Enoch Sontonga**, a teacher at a Methodist mission school in Johannesburg, composed the original 'Nkosi Sikelel' iAfrika', which means 'God bless Africa', in isiXhosa in 1897. In 1927, Samuel Mqhayi, a poet, added seven additional isiXhosa stanzas, and Moses Mphahlele published a Sesotho version in 1942.

- The first person to have the song recorded (in London in 1923) was Solomon T Plaatje, a famous writer and a founding member of the ANC.

- On 20 April 1994, the state president issued a proclamation in which it was stipulated that both 'Nkosi Sikelel' iAfrika' and 'Die Stem van Suid-Afrika' would be the national anthems of South Africa. In 1996 a shortened, combined version of the two anthems was released as the new national anthem, and a part of 'The Call of South Africa' was also incorporated.

- **CJ Langenhoven**, a well-known Afrikaans writer, poet and senator (who also wrote the first Afrikaans science fiction and detective stories!) wrote the words for 'Die Stem van Suid-Afrika' in 1918. A Dutch Reformed Church dominee, ML de Villiers, wrote the music in 1921.

- 'Die Stem van Suid-Afrika' was first sung in public when the national flag was officially hoisted on 31 May 1928, but the announcement that it was accepted as South Africa's national anthem was only made nearly 19 years later, on 2 May 1957.

- The English version, 'The Call of South Africa', was accepted for official use in 1952.

Nkosi Sikelel' iAfrika

Classic Xhosa	English translation	Current Xhosa version
	(Original Lovedale)	
Nkosi, Sikelel' iAfrika;	Lord, bless Africa;	Nkosi Sikelel' iAfrika
Malupakam'upondo lwayo;	May her horn rise high up;	Maluphakanyisw' uphondo lwayo
Yiva imitandazo yetu	Hear Thou our prayers and bless us.	Yiva imathandazo yethu
Usisikelele.		Nkosi Sikelela Nkosi Sikelela
	Chorus	Nkosi Sikelel' iAfrika
Chorus	Descend, O Spirit,	Maluphakanyisw' uphondo lwayo
Yihla Moya, Yihla Moya,	Descend, O Holy Spirit.	Yiva imathandazo yethu
Yihla Moya Oyingcwele.		Nkosi Sikelela
	Bless our chiefs;	Thina lusapho lwayo.
Sikelela iNkosi zetu;	May they remember their Creator,	
Zimkumbule umDali wazo;	Fear Him and revere Him,	**Chorus**
Zimoyike zezimhlouele,	That He may bless them.	Yihla moya, yihla moya
Azisikelele.		Yihla moya oyingcwele
	Bless the public men,	Nkosi Sikelela
Sikelel' amadol' esizwe,	Bless also the youth,	Thina lusapho lwayo.
Sikelela kwa nomlisela	That they may carry the land with	(Repeat)
Ulitwal'ilizwe ngomonde,	patience	
Uwusikilele.	and that Thou mayst bless them.	
Sikelel'amakosikazi;	Bless the wives	
Nawo onk'amanenekazi;	And also all young women;	
Pakamisa wonk'umtinjana	Lift up all the young girls	
Uwusikilele.	And bless them.	
Sikelela abafundisi	Bless the ministers	
Bemvaba zonke zelilizwe;	of all the churches of this land;	
Ubatwese ngoMoya Wako	Endue them with Thy Spirit	
Ubasikelele.	And bless them.	
Sikelel'ulimo nemfuyo;	Bless agriculture and stock-raising;	
Gxota zonk'indlala nezifo;	Banish all famine and diseases;	
Zalisa ilizwe ngempilo	Fill the land with good health	
Ulisikelele.	And bless it.	
Sikelel'amalinga etu	Bless our efforts	
Awomanyana nokuzaka,	of union and self-uplift,	
Awemfundo nemvisiswano	Of education and mutual understanding,	
Uwasikelele.	And bless them.	
Nkosi Sikelel' iAfrika;	Lord, bless Africa;	
Cima bonk' ubugwenxa bayo	Blot out all its wickedness	
Nezigqito, nezono zayo	And its transgressions and sins,	
Uyisikelele.	And bless it.	

Nkosi Sikelel' iAfrika

Sesotho version	Zulu version	Current English version	Afrikaans version
Morena boloka sechaba sa heso	Nkosi, sikelel' iAfrika,	Lord, bless Africa,	Seën ons, Here God,
O fedise dintwa le matshwenyeho,	Maluphakanyisw' udumo lwayo;	May her spirit rise high up.	seën Afrika,
Morena boloka sechaba sa heso,	Yizwa imithandazo yethu	Hear thou our prayers,	Laat sy mag tot in die hemel reik.
O fedise dintwa le matshwenyeho.	Nkosi sikelela,	Lord, bless us.	Hoor ons as ons in gebede vra:
Se boloke, o se boloke,	Nkosi sikelela,	Lord, bless Africa,	Seën ons in Afrika,
O se boloke, o se boloke.	Nkosi, sikelel' iAfrika,	May her spirit rise high up.	Kinders van Afrika.
Sechaba sa heso, Sechaba sa heso.	Maluphakanyisw' udumo lwayo;	Hear thou our prayers,	Daal neer, o Gees,
O se boloke morena se boloke,	Yizwa imithandazo yethu.	Lord, bless us, Your family.	Heilige Gees,
O se boloke sechaba, se boloke.		**Chorus**	Daal neer, o Gees,
Sechaba sa heso, sechaba sa heso.	**Chorus**	Descend, O Spirit,	Heilige Gees,
	Nkosi sikelela,	Descend, O Holy Spirit.	Kom woon in ons,
Chorus	Nkosi sikelela,	Lord, bless us,	Lei ons, o Heilige Gees.
Ma kube njalo! Ma kube njalo!	Woza Moya (woza, woza),	Your family.	
Kude kube ngunaphakade.	Woza Moya (woza, woza),	(Repeat)	Hou u hand, o Heer, oor Afrika,
Kude kube ngunaphakade!	Woza Moya, Oyingcwele.		Lei ons tot by eenheid en begrip,
	Usisikelele,		Hoor ons as ons U om vrede vra.
	Thina lusapho lwayo.		Seën ons in Afrika,
			Kinders van Afrika.
			Seën ons, Here God, seën Afrika,
			Neem dan nou die boosheid van ons weg,
			Maak ons van ons sonde ewig vry.
			Seën ons in Afrika,
			Kinders van Afrika.

Die Stem van Suid Afrika

Uit die blou van onse hemel, uit die diepte van ons see,
Oor ons ewige gebergtes waar die kranse antwoord gee,
Deur ons ver verlate vlaktes met die kreun van ossewa –
Ruis die stem van ons geliefde, van ons land Suid-Afrika.

Ons sal antwoord op jou roepstem, ons sal offer wat jy vra:
Ons sal lewe, ons sal sterwe – ons vir jou, Suid Afrika.

In die merg van ons gebeente, in ons hart en siel en gees,
In ons roem op ons verlede, in ons hoop op wat sal wees,
In ons wil en werk en wandel, van ons wieg tot aan ons graf –
Deel geen ander land ons liefde, trek geen ander trou ons af.

Vaderland! Ons sal die adel van jou naam met ere dra:
Waar en trou as Afrikaners – kinders van Suid-Afrika.

In die songloed van ons somer, in ons winternag se kou,
In die lente van ons liefde, in die lanfer van ons rou,
By die klink van huweliksklokkies, by die kluitklap op die kis –
Streel jou stem ons nooit verniet nie, weet jy waar jou kinders is.

Op jou roep sê ons nooit nee nie, sê ons altyd, altyd ja:
Om te lewe, om te sterwe – ja, ons kom, Suid-Afrika.

Op u almag vas vertrouend het ons vadere gebou:
Skenk ook ons die krag, o Here! om te handhaaf en te hou –
Dat die erwe van ons vaad're vir ons kinders erwe bly:
Knegte van die Allerhoogste, teen die hele wêreld vry.

Soos ons vadere vertrou het, leer ook ons vertrou, o Heer:
Met ons land en met ons nasie sal dit wel wees, God regeer.

CENSUS IN SOUTH AFRICA

Did you know?

- The word *census* dates from the early 17th century, and comes from the Latin *censere*, which means 'to appraise' or 'to assess'. It is also the source of the English words 'censor' and 'censure'. The original meaning referred to 'tax', because in ancient Rome a registration of the population and their property was used for assessing taxes.
- The first official census in South Africa was conducted in the Cape Colony on 5 March 1865, in terms of a census Act passed the previous year.
- In preparation for the 2001 census, South Africa was divided into about 80 000 counting areas, containing between 150 and 250 households each.
- Statistics South Africa recruited more than 86 000 enumerators or census takers.
- South Africa's total population, according to the 1996 census, was 40,58 million.
- South Africa's total population, according to the 2001 census, was 44,8 million.

The Call of South Africa

Ringing out from our blue heavens, from our deep seas breaking round;
Over everlasting mountains where the echoing crags resound;
From our plains where creaking wagons cut their trails into the earth –
Calls the spirit of our Country, of the land that gave us birth.

At thy call we shall not falter, firm and steadfast we shall stand,
At thy will to live or perish, O South Africa, dear land.

In our body and our spirit, in our inmost heart held fast;
In the promise of our future and the glory of the past;
In our will, our work, our striving, from the cradle to the grave –
There's no land that shares our loving, and no bond that can enslave.

Thou hast borne us and we know thee. May our deeds to all proclaim
Our enduring love and service to thy honour and thy name.

In the golden warmth of summer, in the chill of winter's air,
In the surging life of springtime, in the autumn of despair;
When the wedding bells are chiming or when those we love depart;
Thou dost know us for thy children and dost take us to thy heart.

Loudly peals the answering chorus: We are thine, and we shall stand,
Be it life or death, to answer to thy call, beloved land.

In Thy power, Almighty, trusting, did our fathers build of old;
Strengthen then, O Lord, their children to defend, to love, to hold –
That the heritage they gave us for our children yet may be;
Bondsmen only of the Highest and before the whole world free.

As our fathers trusted humbly, teach us, Lord, to trust Thee still;
Guard our land and guide our people in Thy way to do Thy will.

Census date	Total population
17 April 1904	5 174 827
7 May 1911	5 972 757
3 May 1921	6 927 403
5 May 1936	9 587 863
7 May 1946	11 415 925
8 May 1951	12 671 452
6 Sept 1960	16 002 797
6 May 1970	21 448 169
6 May 1980	25 016 525
5 March 1985	23 385 645
7 March 1991	41 733 424
10 October 1996	40 583 573
9, 10 October 2001	44 800 000

- According to mid-year estimates for South Africa, the country's population would have been 45 454 000 in 2002, and 46 430 000 in 2003.

NATIONAL EMBLEMS

Emblem	Name	Scientific name
National animal	Springbok	*Antidorcas marsupialis*
National bird	Blue crane	*Anthropoides paradisia*
National fish	Galjoen	*Coracinus capensis*
National flower	Giant or King Protea	*Protea cynaroides*
National tree	Real Yellowwood	*Podocarpus latifolius*

NATIONAL ANIMAL: SPRINGBOK
(Antidorcas marsupialis)

- The springbok is a small antelope, standing about 75 cm high, and weighing 40 kg. The ram's horns are thicker and rougher than those of the female.
- Springboks can be found in dry areas and open grassland, especially in the Free State, North West, Karoo and up to the West Coast.
- They live in large herds in summer, but move around in smaller herds during winter.
- They eat grass and leaves, and get most of their moisture from eating succulents, wild watermelons and cucumbers, and digging up shallow roots and bulbs.
- Springbok can also drink water with a mineral content too high for other animals.
- The word 'marsupialis' in the Latin name *Antidorcas marsupialis* means 'pouch', and refers to the 10-cm pouch or crest that is hidden under two folds of scent-secreting skin on the back and hind parts of the springbok.
- The springbok can unfold this bag or crest, spreading the white bristles in it, and giving off its typical scent. This is most often done when it is in a state of excitement, and the display is usually accompanied by leaps.
- These leaps are part of a typical jumping display, known as 'pronking', which can also be described as slow bounces, which allow it to jump 2 to 4 m high, and as far as 15 m. Other members of the herd will follow this example.

NATIONAL BIRD: BLUE CRANE
(Anthropoides paradisia)

- The blue crane is approximately one metre high, and almost exclusive to South Africa. Some stray into Botswana, Lesotho and Swaziland, and there is also an isolated breeding group at Namibia's Etosha Pan.
- The name *Anthropoides paradisia* means 'man-like' and 'paradise'. They are also known as 'paradise cranes' or Stanley cranes.

- This regal bird has a light blue-grey colour, a long neck, a largish, round head and elegant wing plumes, which reach the ground.
- Blue cranes can usually be found in pairs or in small families. They are fairly common in the Karoo, but also favour the grasslands of KwaZulu-Natal and the highveld.
- They eat seeds, insects and reptiles, and lay their eggs (usually two at a time) in the bare veld, often close to water.
- Although the blue crane is usually quiet, it does have a distinctive, rattling, fairly high-pitched cry or croak, which can be heard far away.
- The blue crane is known as 'indwe' in isiXhosa, and its extended tertiary feathers adorned warriors' heads during the Frontier Wars.

NATIONAL FISH: GALJOEN
(Coracinus capensis)

- The galjoen is found only along the coast of southern Africa, usually in shallow water, often in rough surf, and sometimes very close to the shore. Its fins are well developed, with prominent spines.
- The record size for a galjoen is more than 55 cm long and 7 kg in weight, although the average fish is much smaller.
- The colour of the galjoen that are found in sandy areas is silver-bronze, but near rocks they are almost completely black. In KwaZulu-Natal the galjoen is known as blackfish or black bream.
- The scientific name *Coracinus* means 'raven', or 'black colour', referring to the galjoen's dark colour.
- Small groups of galjoen can usually be found off rocky shores, gullies and kelp beds, where they eat red and coraline seaweed, but more commonly red bait, small mussels and barnacles, which make up about 75% of its diet.
- The suggestion to make the galjoen South Africa's national fish came from the late Margaret Smith, wife of the famous ichthyologist JLB Smith, and a director of the JLB Smith Institute of Ichthyology in Grahamstown. In the 1950 version of *The Sea Fishes of Southern Africa* by JLB Smith, the following is said of the galjoen: 'Probably the first typical fish to be noticed by the earlier settlers. It might well be selected as a marine emblem to rank with the Springbok and the Protea.'

NATIONAL FLOWER: GIANT OR
KING PROTEA *(Protea cynaroides)*

- The King Protea, also known as the Giant Protea, can be found over a wide area in the south-western and southern parts of the Western Cape, as well as in the Eastern Cape, from the Cederberg to just east of Grahamstown.
- *Cynaroides* means 'like cynara' [artichoke], because the flower heads of the King Protea look like artichokes.
- The King Protea is the largest in the genus, and its flower head can measure 30 cm across.
- A number of different varieties in colour and leaf shapes are found, but the well-known pink flower is regarded as the most beautiful.
- The proteas were named after the Greek god Proteus, the son of Poseidon, the god of the sea. Proteus knew all things past, present and future, but he could change his shape at will to avoid the prophesying. He assumed shapes of wild animals and monsters.
- In South Africa, 85 of the 115 species of protea are found in the Western Cape.
- The King Protea is South Africa's national sport emblem. It appears on the jerseys of the Springbok rugby players, the caps and shirts of the national cricket team, and it is the name of the national netball team.

NATIONAL TREE: REAL YELLOWWOOD
(Podocarpus latifolius)

- The yellowwood family has been present in the southern part of Africa for more than 100 million years.
- The Real Yellowwood is the most common of the South African yellowwoods, occurring from Table Mountain in the Western Cape, along the southern and eastern Cape coast, in the Drakensberg ravines, and up to the Soutpansberg and the Blouberg in Limpopo, through to Swaziland.
- It grows in evergreen forests and patches of mountain forest, as well as on exposed mountainsides.
- The Real Yellowwood tree's bark is khaki-coloured to grey when it is old, when it becomes deeply split and peels off in strips.
- The crown is small in relation to its height, and often covered with grey lichen. It has white, light green or pink male and female cones, which resemble pine cones.
- Male cones are about 25 mm long and are usually solitary. The seed, which has the shape and colour of a cherry, develops on the female cone.

- The generic name *Podocarpus* means 'seed with a foot', referring to the seed being attached to a red fruit to attract birds.
- The specific Latin name *latifolius* means 'broad leaf'.
- The trees in yellowwood forests can grow as high as 40 m, and the base of the trunk can be as much as 3 m in diameter.
- Yellowwood trees in unsheltered places (like the slopes of mountains) are usually gnarled, short and bushy.
- New leaves are light green or bronze in colour, becoming bluish-green with age. The adult leaves will be about 90 mm long and 6–12 mm wide.
- The wood of the Real Yellowwood was used extensively for building houses and ships, and even for railway sleepers. It is still used in boat building, as flooring and in the manufacture of furniture, in spite of the fact that it is spirally grained and tends to warp.

SOUTH AFRICAN SPORTS TEAM NICKNAMES

Rugby team	Springboks
Rugby team (1995 World Cup)	AmaBokoboko
Men's soccer team	Bafana Bafana
Women's soccer team	Banyana Banyana
Under-23 soccer team	AmaGlug-glug
Under-20 soccer team	Amajitas
Under-19 women's soccer team	Basetsane
Under-17 soccer team	Tornadoes
Cricket team	Proteas
Netball team	Proteas
Paralympic team	AmaKrokokroko
Women's hockey team	Easi Ntombis

─── SOUTH AFRICA SPORTING NICKNAMES ───

Name	Nickame	Sport
Dingaan Thobela	Rose of Soweto	Boxing
Francois Botha	White Buffalo	Boxing
Gerrie Coetzee	The Boksburg Bomber	Boxing
Jacob Matlala	Baby Jake	Boxing
Kallie Knoetze	Die Bek van Boomstraat	Boxing
Lehlohonolo Ledwaba	Hands of Stone	Boxing
Masibulele Makepula	Hawk	Boxing
Mpush Makambi	Lion King	Boxing
Peter Mathebula	Terror	Boxing
Thulani Malinga	Sugarboy	Boxing
Willie Maqolo	Wee Willie Wele	Boxing
Zolani Petelo	The Tiger	Boxing
Vuyani Bungu	The Beast	Boxing
Allan Donald	White Lightning	Cricket
Herschelle Gibbs	Scooter	Cricket
Lance Klusener	Zulu	Cricket
Mark Boucher	Guinness	Cricket
Shaun Pollock	Ginger Ninja	Cricket
Hugh Tayfield	Toey	Cricket
Gary Kirsten	Gazza	Cricket
Herbert Roy Lance	Tiger	Cricket
Paul Adams	Gogga	Cricket
Graeme Smith	Biff	Cricket
Ernie Els	The Big Easy	Golf
Gary Player	The Black Knight	Golf
Harold Henning	The Horse	Golf
Retief Goosen	The Goose	Golf
Michael Leonard Roberts	Muis	Horse racing
April Phumo	Styles	Soccer
Ephraim Mashaba	Shakes	Soccer
Irvin Khoza	Iron Duke	Soccer
Jomo Sono	The Black Prince	Soccer
John Moshoeu	Shoes	Soccer
Solomon Morewa	Stix	Soccer
Phil Masinga	Chippa	Soccer
Lucas Radebe	Rhoo	Soccer
Karen Muir	Timid Torpedo	Swimming
Amanda Coetzer	Little Assassin	Tennis
Pieter du Randt	Os	Rugby
Danie Craven	Bie-Bie/Dok	Rugby
Werner Swanepoel	Smiley	Rugby
Pieter Rossouw	Slap Tjips	Rugby
James Dalton	Bullet	Rugby
Johannes Conradie	Bolla	Rugby

SOUTH AFRICA'S GOLFING MASTERS

∾ GARY PLAYER ∾

In 1965 Gary Player became only the third golfer in history – after Ben Hogan and Gene Sarazen – to win all four of the Grand Slam tournaments (the US PGA, the US Open, the US Masters and the British Open). Player won the four Majors in the following years:

- British Open: 1959, 1968,1974
- US Open: 1965
- US Masters: 1961, 1974, 1978
- US PGA: 1962, 1972

He also won the following big titles:

- World Matchplay Tournament: 1965, 1966, 1968, 1971, 1973
- Australian Open: 1958, 1962, 1963, 1965, 1969, 1970,1974
- South African Open: 1956, 1960, 1965–1969, 1972, 1975–1977, 1979, 1981

Did you know?

- Gary Player's second name is Jim, and he was nicknamed 'The Black Knight', because he always wore black.
- He was the top money earner in the USA in 1961, with a grand total of $64 540.
- In 1965 he won the US Open, the World Golf Series, the individual and team prize (with Harold Henning) in the World Tournament, the World Matchplay title and the Australian Open.
- Player was named South Africa's Sportsman of the Century at the end of the 20th century.

∾ BOBBY LOCKE ∾

Bobby Locke won the British Open four times in eight years: in 1949, 1950, 1952 and 1957.

He also won the SA Amateur and SA Open titles at the age of 17, and won the SA Open title a total of nine times.

Did you know?

- Bobby Locke's birth names were Arthur D'Arcy.

∾ ERNIE ELS ∾

In 1994 Ernie Els became only the fourth non-American to win the US Open Golf title since 1911. (The other three were Tommy Armour, UK, 1927; Gary Player, SA, 1965; David Graham, Australia, 1981.) Els repeated this feat in 1997, and added the British Open title in 2002. He also won the World Matchplay title from 1994 to 1996, and repeated this victory twice more – in 2002 and 2003.

Did you know?
• Ernie Els is nicknamed 'The Big Easy'. He was born Ernest Theodore in 1969.

∾ RETIEF GOOSEN ∾

Retief Goosen, nicknamed 'The Goose', was born in Pietersburg (now Polokwane), and won the US Open title in a play-off at Southern Hills in 2001, and again at Shinnecock Hills in 2004. He was also first on the European Order of Merit in 2001 and 2002, won the World Cup team title with Ernie Els in 2001, and produced five top-10 finishes in his first 11 tournaments on the 2004 PGA Tour before winning the US Open title.

——— CLIMATE AND RAINFALL ———

Temperature and rainfall data for the period 1961–1990									
			TEMPERATURE				RAINFALL		
City/Town	Position	Height (m)	Highest recorded	Ave. daily maximum	Ave. daily minimum	Lowest recorded	Average annual (mm)	Average days with ≥ 1 mm	Highest 24-hour rain-fall (mm)
Cape Town	33° 59' S 18° 36' E	42	41	22	11	−1	515	103	65
Johannesburg	26° 08' S 28° 14' E	1 763	35	22	10	−8	713	99	188
Pretoria	25° 44' S 28° 11' E	1 330	36	25	12	−6	674	87	160
East London	33° 02' S 27° 50' E	125	42	23	14	3	921	121	447
Port Elizabeth	33° 59' S 25° 36' E	60	41	22	14	−1	624	112	429
Bloemfontein	29° 06' S 26° 18' E	1 351	39	24	8	−10	559	84	142
Durban	29° 58' S 30° 57' E	8	40	25	17	3	1 009	130	197
Richards Bay	28° 48' S 32° 06' E	47	43	26	17	4	1 228	113	317
Pietermaritzburg	29° 36' S 30° 26' E	613	42	26	11	−4	844	138	225
Nelspruit	25° 26' S 30° 59' E	671	40	27	13	−2	767	100	130
Polokwane	23° 52' S 29° 27' E	1 230	37	25	12	−4	478	65	79
Mmabatho	25° 47' S 25° 32' E	1 281	40	27	12	−6	539	72	99
Kimberley	28° 48' S 24° 46' E	1 198	40	26	11	−8	414	71	88
Upington	28° 24' S 21° 16' E	836	43	29	13	−7	189	37	59
George	34° 00' S 22° 23' E	193	41	21	11	0	715	121	132
Beaufort West	32° 21' S 22° 36' E	842	41	25	10	−6	236	43	83

——— WATER ... ———

- is a tasteless, odourless liquid with a bluish tint that can be seen in very deep layers.
- is at its maximum density at 4 °C (39 °F).
- has a freezing point of 0 °C (32 °F) and a boiling point of 100 °C (212 °F) at Standard Atmospheric Pressure (760 mm of mercury).
- is the only substance that occurs in all three states – liquid, gas and solid – at ordinary temperatures.
- is used in the metric system to define the gram.
- has the chemical formula H_2O, which means that it consists of hydrogen and oxygen, with one atom of oxygen for every two of hydrogen.

A world of water
- Water covers 75% of the Earth's surface.
- The world's oceans contain 97,5% of the Earth's water.
- The land has only 2,4% of the world's water.
- The atmosphere holds less than 0,001% of all the world's water.
- Just 1% of the Earth's water is available for drinking.
- Almost 2% of the water on Earth is frozen.
- The world's average rainfall is 860 mm.

Ice
- Melting ice remains at a constant 0 °C (32 °F).
- Ice is less dense than water at 0 °C (32 °F).
- Water can remain liquid even below its freezing point, up to –25 °C, provided it is not disturbed, the temperature does not drop further and nothing is added to it.
- Ice is used in refrigerators because it has strong hydrogen bonds, and takes more energy to melt than most other substances.
- A mass of ice occupies 9% more volume than an equal mass of water, which can cause water pipes to burst when the water in them freezes.
- When water enters little cracks in a rock and freezes, the expansion creates so much pressure that the rock could split.
- Ice floats because it is less dense than water. This means that ice in rivers, lakes and oceans traps the warmer water below, and allows fish and other water creatures to survive the freezing temperatures of the surface.

Water in living beings

- Blood in animals and sap in plants is mostly water.
- Between 50% and 90% of the weight of living organisms is made up of water.
- An adult human body is composed of about 55–60% water.
- The human body's brain and skin is 70% water, its blood is 82% water, and the lungs are nearly 90% water.
- You can survive about a month without food, but only five to seven days without water.

More water facts

- It is possible to drink water today that was here in the time of the dinosaurs.
- The average urban home, which has 4,6 people, can use 640 ℓ of water per day.
- A dripping tap can waste as much as 60 ℓ per day, which is 1 800 ℓ per month and 21 900 ℓ per year.
- A toilet is the biggest user of indoor water. It uses an average of 11 ℓ of water when it is flushed.
- A leaking toilet can waste up to 100 000 ℓ of water per year, which is enough for three full baths every day.
- The average bath holds between 150 and 200 ℓ of water when filled to the brim.
- It takes about 2,5 ℓ of water to cook pasta and about 5 ℓ to clean the pot.

SOUTH AFRICA'S LONGEST RIVERS

	River	Length (km)
1	Orange	2 340
2	Limpopo	1 600
3	Vaal	1 160
4	Olifants (tributary of Limpopo)	760
5	Tugela	520
6	Pongola	440
7	Mzimkulu	380
8	Mzimvubu	320
9	Caledon	315
10	Breede	310

SOUTH AFRICA'S LARGEST DAMS

Dam	Full capacity (million m³)	River
Gariep	5 341	Orange
Vanderkloof	3 171	Orange
Sterkfontein	2 616	Nuwejaarspruit
Nuwejaarspruit Vaal	2 603	Vaal
Pongolapoort	2 445	Pongolo
Bloemhof	1 264	Vaal
Theewaterskloof	480	Sonderend
Heyshope	451	Assegaai
Woodstock	380	Tugela
Loskop	361	Olifants
Grootdraai	354	Vaal
Kalkfontein	318	Riet
Goedertrouw	304	Mhlatuze
Albert Falls	288	Mgeni
Brandvlei	284	Smalblaar/Holsloot
Spioenkop	277	Tugela
Umtata	253	Mtata
Driekoppies	250	Lomati
Inanda	241	Mgeni
Hartbeespoort	212	Crocodile
Erfenis	207	Groot Vet
Rhenosterkop	204	Elands
Molatedi	200	Groot Marico
Ntshingwayo	198	Ngagane
Zaaihoek	192	Slang
Midmar	175	Mgeni

Total storage capacity per province

Province	Capacity (million m³)
Eastern Cape	1 719,8
Free State	13 448,8
Gauteng	2 644,6
Kwazulu-Natal	4 707,0
Limpopo	813,8
Mpumalanga	2 647,3
North West	772,0
Northern Cape	141,4
Western Cape	1 647,7
Total	**28 542,4**

Name changes of some well-known dams

New name	Old name
Kwena	Braam Raubenheimer
Impofu	Charlie Malan
Tzaneen	Fanie Botha
Mokolo	Hans Strijdom
Gariep	Hendrik Verwoerd
Nsami	Hudson Ntsanwisi
Klaserie	Jan Wassenaar
Lake Mentz	Darlington
Arabie	Mokgomo Matlala
Kouga	Paul Sauer
Vanderkloof	PK le Roux
Orange-Riet Canal	Sarel Hayward Canal

TEMPERATURE SCALES

Name	Symbol	Melting point of water	Boiling point of water	History
Fahrenheit	°F	32	212	The German scientist Daniel Fahrenheit established 0 °F as the temperature where equal amounts of ice, water and salt are mixed. He then chose 96 °F as the temperature 'when the thermometer is held in the mouth or under the armpit of a living man in good health'. The 32 and 212 were later determined from the original definitions. 0 °F corresponds to about −17,8 °C and about 255,4K.
Celsius	°C	0	100	The Swedish astronomer Anders Celsius chose 0 and 100 arbitrarily for the melting and boiling points of water at a standard sea-level air pressure (it was originally the other way round, but Carl Linnaeus suggested the switch). 0 °C corresponds to 32 °F and 273,16K.
Kelvin	K	273,16	373,16	This scale was named after the British scientist Lord Kelvin, Baron Kelvin of Largs (William Thompson). It is based upon the definitions of the Centigrade scale and experimental evidence that absolute zero is −273,16 °C. Zero Kelvin is the lowest possible temperature, at which not even atoms move around any more. Zero Kelvin corresponds to −273,16 °and to −459,67 °F.
Rankine	°r	491,67	671,67	This scale is named after the Scottish engineer and physicist William John Macquorn Rankine, and is based on the definitions of the Fahrenheit scale and experimental evidence that absolute zero is −273,16 °C. Rankine zero is absolute zero, but Fahrenheit degrees are used.
Réaumur	°R	0	80	Named after René Antoine Ferchault de Réaumur, who first proposed it in 1731.

Did you know?
* To convert a temperature:
    - From Celsius to Fahrenheit: Multiply the Celsius value by 1,8 and then add 32.
    - From Fahrenheit to Celsius: Subtract 32 from the Fahrenheit value and divide by 1,8.
* The only temperature where the readings on a Fahrenheit thermometer and a Celsius thermometer will be equal is –40 °. (In other words, –40 °F = –40 °C.)

RICHTER MAGNITUDE SCALE

The American seismologist Charles Francis Richter (1900–1985) developed the Richter scale in 1935. It was initially used to measure earthquakes in California, but was later expanded for use all over the world. The scale is based on the logarithm of the amplitude of waves measured by a seismometer, and measures how much the ground shakes 100 km from the epicentre of the earthquake. Each whole number indicates a tenfold increase in amplitude, while the energy released is about 31 times more.

Magnitude	Description	Effect
1	Not felt by people	Recordable on seismometers
2	Not felt by many people	Recordable on seismometers
3	Minor quake	Felt by many people, but not causing significant damage
4	Minor quake	Felt by many people, but causing little or no damage
5	Moderate quake	Felt over wide area, may cause local damage
6	Strong quake (destructive)	Can cause damage 10s of km from source
7	Major earthquake	Can cause damage up to 100 km from epicentre
8	Great earthquake	Can cause damage up to 100s of km from epicentre
9	Great earthquake (extremely rare)	Causes damage, and effects can be felt 1 000 km from epicentre

MERCALLI INTENSITY SCALE

Giuseppe Mercalli (1850–1914), an Italian seismologist, devised this scale in 1902, to relate the intensity of an earthquake and the effects experienced locally, as well as the role of the local environment. It is measured from I to XII, and both describes and rates earthquakes in terms of human reactions and observations.

Magnitude	Name	Description of effects
I	Instrumental	Not felt at all by humans; detected only by seismographic instruments.
II	Feeble	Felt only by a few people; slight swaying of tall buildings could be noticed.
III	Slight	Could be experienced by people indoors, but very little other effect.
IV	Moderate	Felt indoors and outdoors. Hanging objects (chandeliers and plants) may swing, parked cars might rock.
V	Rather strong	Strong enough to waken sleepers and cause objects to fall from shelves and break.
VI	Strong	Felt by everyone. Stronger shaking, can cause people to fall over and walls and ceilings to crack.
VII	Very strong	People find it difficult to stand. Loose bricks can fall, people fall over, damage to poorly constructed buildings. Waves may be seen in ponds and swimming pools.
VIII	Destructive	Tall buildings sway, furniture breaks, cars swerve.
IX	Ruinous	General panic. The ground cracks, well-constructed buildings damaged, underground pipes break.
X	Disastrous	Landslides, buildings fall, ground cracks widely.
XI	Very disastrous	Many buildings collapse. Bridges and buildings are destroyed, large fissures open, rail tracks buckle.
XII	Catastrophic	Virtually total destruction. Rocks moved, objects thrown about.

Did you know?
• Another earthquake intensity scale is the Rossi-Forel scale, named after Michele Stefano Conte de Rossi and François-Alphonse Forel.

EARTHQUAKES IN SOUTH AFRICA

The first report of earthquakes in South Africa was in 1620, when two ships that were anchored at Robben Island reported a few thunderclaps like cannon shots. Although there were other reports of earthquakes in the next few centuries, the first really notable tremors occurred over a period of eight days in 1809. Over the next nearly two centuries a handful of strong earthquakes were felt in South Africa.

Date	Place	Description	Intensity (Mercalli)	Magnitude (Richter)
4–12 December 1809	Cape Town	Three strong quakes. All buildings suffer cracks, water spouts in places.	VI–VIII	6,1
2 June 1811	Cape Town	Two loud reports and shocks. The second is about as strong as the first shock of 4 December 1809. Walls cracked.	VII	5,5–6
Early 1826	Saldanha Bay	Severe tremor.	VI	± 5
20 February 1912	Koffiefontein	The quake is felt all over South Africa, and many farm buildings are completely destroyed.	VIII	± 6
4 December 1920	Cape Province	Very strong quake in the sea, felt from Cape Town to George and Port Elizabeth.	IV	6,2
9 October 1921	Tulbagh	A strong quake, which shook houses, and caused slight damage to some.	VI	± 5,0
18 November 1932	Cape Town	Fairly strong.	VI	± 5
31 December 1932	Off St Lucia	One or two buildings collapse, cracks and fissures appear in ground.	VIII	6,0–6,5
27 August 1963	Western Cape	A sharp shock; felt all over Western Cape, especially in De Doorns–Worcester–Ceres area. A few walls cracked.	VI	5,0
29 September 1969	Western Cape	The worst shock is felt in Ceres, Tulbagh and Wolseley. Extensive damage is caused to certain buildings, with total destruction of old and poorly constructed buildings. The shock causes water spouts, mountain fires and extensive cracks. This quake was felt 1 175 km far. Twelve people were killed and many injured.	VIII–IX	6,3
14 April 1970	Western Cape	Felt especially at Ceres and Tulbagh; further damage is caused.	VII	5,7
8 December 1976	Welkom	Extensive damage is caused to many buildings, and windows were broken. A block of flats, six stories high, collapsed after the event.	VII	5,2
7 March 1992	Carletonville	The high population density around the epicentre caused an unusual amount of damage. Houses as far as Pretoria were damaged.	VII	4,7

Did you know?

• San Francisco is prone to earthquakes, because it lies on the San Andreas Fault, the geological fault zone in California, which stretches north-west for about 970 km. In the early hours of 18 April 1906, this city experienced the most devastating earthquake in the history of the United States. It was later estimated that the quake measured as high as 8,25 on the Richter scale. The tremor lasted only a minute, but more than 3 000 people died as a result of the fires it caused, while 225 000 were injured and as many as 200 000 of the city's 350 000 inhabitants were left homeless. The damage to property was more than $400 000 000. The earthquake caused the ground to break open along the fault for a distance of nearly 440 km, and in one place the displacement was 6,4 m.

• *The Times* of 20 April 1906 included this description of the force with which the earthquake struck: 'The Cliff House, a massive hotel built of stone and standing on solid rock, well-known to visitors who go out there to watch the sea-lions basking underneath on the rocks, has been hurled bodily into the sea and left not a vestige behind.'

• The earthquake that hit Tangshan in China on 27 July 1976 resulted in 255 000 deaths. This was the official death toll, although the estimated death toll could be as high as 655 000.

• According to the US Geological Survey National Earthquake Information Center, the largest earthquake (by magnitude) since 1900 occurred in southern Chile on 22 May 1960, registering 9,5 on the Richter scale. Between 4 000 and 5 000 people died in this quake. An earthquake in Prince William Sound, Alaska, on 28 March 1964 reached a magnitude of 9,0; a tremor in the Andreanof Islands, Aleutian Islands, on 9 March 1957 was measured at 9,1; and one on the Kamchatka Peninsula on 4 November 1952 registered 9,0 on the Richter scale.

GLASGOW COMA SCALE

The Glasgow coma scale (GCS) is the most widely used scoring system for quantifying the level of consciousness following a traumatic brain injury.

Best eye response (4)	Best verbal response (5)	Best motor response (6)
1 No eye opening	1 No verbal response	1 No motor response
2 Eye opening to pain	2 Incomprehensible sounds	2 Extension to pain
3 Eye opening to verbal command	3 Inappropriate words	3 Flexion to pain
4 Eyes open spontaneously	4 Confused	4 Withdrawal from pain
	5 Orientated	5 Localising pain
		6 Obeys commands

Did you know?

- The GCS score can be between 3 and 15, of which 3 is the worst and 15 the best.
- The phrase 'GCS of 11' is always broken down into its different components to give a more accurate summary of the situation (e.g. E3V3M5 = GCS 11).
- A GCS of 8 or less indicates a severe brain injury.
- A GCS of 9 to 12 indicates a moderate injury.
- A GCS of 13 indicates a mild brain injury.

NB: Factors such as drug use, alcohol intoxication, shock, hypoxemia or metabolic disturbances could alter the GCS independently of the brain trauma.

A FEW MORE SCALES

Name	It measures ...
Scoville scale	Chilli pepper heat
Ringelmann scale	Darkness of smoke
Balling scale	Density of liquids
Baumé scale	Density of liquids
Twaddell scale	Density of liquids
Mohs' scale	Hardness of minerals
Guttman scale	Mental attitudes
Pythagorean scale	Musical pitch
Forel scale	Ocean and lake water colour
Holmes scale	Psychological stress
Linke scale	Shades of blue (of the sky)

CHRIS BARNARD

- Christiaan Neethling Barnard, the South African surgeon who performed the first human heart transplant in 1967, was born in Beaufort West on 8 November 1922, as one of four sons. His father was a minister of religion.
- Barnard studied at the University of Cape Town, and received his degree in 1953. He also studied at the University of Minnesota in Minneapolis, receiving his master of science in surgery in 1958. In the same year he received his doctorate in philosophy.
- When Barnard returned to the University of Cape Town in 1958, he taught surgery, specialised in open-heart surgery, and designed artificial heart valves.
- On 3 December 1967 he performed the first human heart transplant, transferring the heart of the 25-year-old Denise Darvall to the chest of Louis Washkansky, a 55-year-old grocer. Washkansky died 18 days later of double pneumonia.

> 'Dr Terry O'Donovan removed the (donor's) heart from the chest and carried it to the adjacent recipient operating room, to which I had returned. Louis Washkansky's heart was then similarly removed, and, for the first time in my life, I stared into an empty chest. At that moment, the full impact of what I was attempting became abundantly clear to me.'
> — CHRIS BARNARD

- The second transplant was on 2 January 1968. The patient was a dentist, Philip Blaiberg, who lived for 563 days after the operation.
- Barnard was head of the cardiac unit of Groote Schuur Hospital in Cape Town until 1983, when he retired from active surgery.
- Chris Barnard achieved some other firsts as well. He did the world's first 'piggy-back' heart transplant on 25 November 1974, in an operation where a donor heart was transplanted, but the patient's own heart was not removed.
- He published 15 books, two of which were autobiographies: *One Life* (1970) and *The Second Life* (1993).
- Christiaan Neethling Barnard died of an acute asthma attack in Phapos, Cyprus, in 2001.

THE NOBEL PRIZE

'Home is where I work and I work everywhere.'
— ALFRED BERNHARD NOBEL (1833–1896)

Nobel was a Swedish chemist, inventor and philanthropist who was born in Stockholm and educated in St Petersburg, Russia, and studied chemistry and technology in France and the United States. He built up companies and laboratories in more than 20 countries all over the world. He invented dynamite and gelignite.

South African recipients of the Nobel Prize			
Recipient	Year	Nobel Prize	Reason for award
Dr Max Theiler, medical researcher	1951	Medicine	For his discoveries concerning yellow fever and how to combat it.
Albert Luthuli, president of the ANC	1960	Peace	For his fight for the ideals expressed in the declaration of human rights embodied in the Charter of the United Nations.
Allan Cormack*	1979	Medicine	For the development of computer-assisted tomography.
Sir Aaron Klug,** medical doctor	1982	Medicine	For his development of crystallographic electron micro-scopy and his structural elucidation of biologically important nucleic acid-protein complexes.

Recipient	Year	Nobel Prize	Reason for award
Desmond Tutu, archbishop	1984	Peace	For his role as a unifying leader figure in the campaign to resolve the problem of apartheid in South Africa.
Nadine Gordimer, author	1991	Literature	Who through her magnificent epic writing has – in the words of Alfred Nobel – been of very great benefit to humanity.
Nelson Mandela, president of the RSA	1993	Peace	For his work for the peaceful termination of the apartheid regime.
FW de Klerk, president of the RSA	1993	Peace	For his work for the peaceful termination of the apartheid regime.
JM Coetzee, author	2003	Literature	Who in innumerable guises portrays the surprising involvement of the outsider.

* Alan M Cormack (1924–1998), who received the Nobel Prize for Medicine in 1979, was born in Johannesburg. He graduated with a master's degree in physics at the University of Cape Town, and later emigrated to the USA, where he died in 1998.

** According to Sir Aaron Klug's autobiography: 'I was born in 1926 to Lazar and Bella (née Silin) Klug in Zelvas, Lithuania, but remember nothing of the place, because I was brought to South Africa as a child of two and grew up there.'

Did you know?

- The six Nobel Prize categories are: Literature, Peace, Physics, Chemistry, Economics, and Medicine and Physiology. The Nobel Prize for Economics was awarded for the first time in 1969.
- Five of the prizes are awarded in Stockholm, Sweden, on the 10th of December, the date when Nobel died. The peace prize is awarded in Oslo, Norway.
- The Nobel Prize for each winner consists of a gold medal, a diploma and an amount of money. In 1901 this amount was about 150 782 Swedish krona, while the amount in 2004 is 10 million Swedish krona (nearly R9 million).
- The Nobel Prize for Economics is the only Nobel Prize that has never been won by a woman.
- William Lawrence Bragg, a physicist from England, was the youngest Nobel Prize winner. He won the Physics Prize in 1915, when he was only 25 years old.
- Three people won the Nobel Prize at the age of 87: American scientist Peyton Rous (Physiology, 1966); Austrian scientist Karl von Frisch (Medicine, 1973); and Polish scientist Joseph Rotblat (Peace, 1995).
- Four people won the Noble Prize twice: Marie Curie (France) for Physics in 1903 and Chemistry in 1911; Linus Pauling (USA) for Chemistry in 1954 and Peace in 1962; John Bardeen (USA) for Physics in 1956 and 1972; and Frederick Sanger (UK) for Chemistry in 1958 and 1980.

Female Nobel Laureates

Only 31 women have received Nobel Prizes, in the following categories.

Physics	2
Chemistry	3
Physiology and Medicine	6
Literature	9
Peace	11
Economics	0

- Nadine Gordimer (Nobel Prize for Literature) is the only South African woman with a Nobel Prize.

Most Nobel Prize winners by country (1901–2003)

	Country	Prizes
1	United States	270
2	United Kingdom	101
3	Germany	76
4	France	49
5	Sweden	30
6	Switzerland	22
7	Netherlands	15
8	USSR	14
9	Italy	14
10	Denmark	13

NADINE GORDIMER

- Nadine Gordimer was born in Springs, South Africa, on 20 November 1923, to Isidore and Nan Gordimer. She received the Nobel Prize for Literature in 1991, and was joint winner of the Booker Prize in 1974 for her novel *The Conservationist*.
- Gordimer received honorary degrees from, among others, Yale, Harvard, Columbia, New School for Social Research (USA); University of Leuven (Belgium); University of York, Cambridge University (England); and the Universities of Cape Town and the Witwatersrand (South Africa). She also received the *Commandeur de l'Ordre des Arts et des Lettres* from France.

'The writer is of service to humankind only insofar as the writer uses the word even against his or her own loyalties, trusts the state of being, as it is revealed, to hold somewhere in its complexity filaments of the cord of truth, able to be bound together, here and there, in art: trusts the state of being to yield somewhere fragmentary phrases of truth, which is the final word of words, never changed by our stumbling efforts to spell it out and write it down, never changed by lies, by semantic sophistry, by the dirtying of the word for the purposes of racism, sexism, prejudice, domination, the glorification of destruction, the curses and the praise-songs.' — NADINE GORDIMER, IN HER NOBEL LECTURE
ON 7 DECEMBER 1991

Nadine Gordimer's major works

Novels	Year	Collections	Year
The Lying Days	1953	Face to Face	1949
A World of Strangers	1958	The Soft Voice of the Serpent	1952
Occasion for Loving	1963	Six Feet of the Country	1956
The Late Bourgeois World	1966	Not for Publication	1965
A Guest of Honour	1970	Livingstone's Companions	1971
The Conservationist	1974	Selected Stories	1975
Burger's Daughter	1979	No Place Like: Selected Stories	1978
July's People	1981	A Soldier's Embrace	1980
A Sport of Nature	1987	Something Out There	1984
My Son's Story	1990	Jump: And Other Stories	1991
None to Accompany Me	1994	Why Haven't You Written?:	
The House Gun	1998	Selected Stories, 1950–1972	1992
The Pickup	2001	Loot: And Other Stories	2003
		Non-fiction	**Year**
		The Essential Gesture	1988
		On the Mines	1973
		The Black Interpreters	1973

JM COETZEE

- JM Coetzee was born in Cape Town on 9 February 1940, and went to school in Cape Town and Worcester. He was a student at the University of Cape Town, where he graduated with honours degrees in English (1960) and mathematics (1961).

- Coetzee went to England from 1962 to 1965 to do research for a thesis on the English novelist Ford Madox Ford, and worked as a computer programmer while he was there.

- He also studied in the USA, and graduated from the University of Texas at Austin with a PhD in English, linguistics and Germanic languages.
- JM Coetzee became the first double winner of Britain's Booker Prize for Fiction, for *Life & Times of Michael K* (1983) and *Disgrace* (1999). He received the Nobel Prize for Literature in 2003.

Did you know?
JM Coetzee was born as John Michael Coetzee, but later changed his middle name to Maxwell.

JM Coetzee's major works			
Novels	**Year**	**Other works**	**Year**
Dusklands	1974	*White Writing: On the Culture of Letters*	1988
In the Heart of the Country	1977	*Doubling the Point : Essays*	
Waiting for the Barbarians	1980	*and Interviews*	1992
Life & Times of Michael K	1983	*Giving Offense: Essays on Censorship*	1996
Foe	1986	*Boyhood: Scenes from Provincial Life*	1997
Age of Iron	1990	*What is Realism?*	1997
The Master of Petersburg	1994	*The Lives of Animals*	1999
Disgrace	1999	*The Humanities in Africa*	2001
Youth	2002	*Stranger Shores: Essays, 1986–1999*	2001
Elizabeth Costello: Eight Lessons	2003		

ISLANDS OFF THE SOUTH AFRICAN COAST

Name	Size (ha)	Position	
Robben Island	574	In Table Bay, 11 km from Cape Town	Home to 74 bird species, and 4 000 African penguins.
Dassen Island	222	9 km from Yzerfontein	Large population of rock hyrax (dassies). Principal home of the African penguin, and a breeding site for white pelicans.
Jutten Island	43	In Saldanha Bay	
Schaapen Island	29	In Saldanha Bay	These islands are the breeding place of 30% of African black oystercatchers. They also house the largest colony of Kelp gulls in South Africa. European rabbits abound on Jutten and Schaapen; on the latter they are mostly albinos.
Bird Island	19	In Lambert's Bay	
Malgas Island	18	In Saldanha Bay	
Marcus Island	17	In Saldanha Bay	
Meeuw Island	7	In Saldanha Bay	
St Croix Island	16	In Algoa Bay, opposite Coega River mouth	60% of the world's African penguins breed here; world's largest colony of Cape gannets live here.
Bird Island	11	In Algoa Bay (on the east side)	

Name	Size (ha)	Position	
Vondeling Island	9	Seaward side of Langebaan Lagoon	
Dyer Island	20	Near Gans Bay	The only known breeding site for Leach's Storm-petrel in the southern hemisphere. Popular for shark cage diving.
Geyser Island	3	Near Gans Bay	Cape Fur seals attract great white sharks.

South Africa's other islands		
Name	Size	Position
Marion Island	290 km²	46°38'S 37°59'E: In the South Atlantic; 2 300 km south-east of Cape Town and 250 km north of Antarctica. It is 24 km long, and the highest point is 1 186 m above sea level.
Prince Edward Islands	44 km²	46°37'S 37°57'E: In the South Atlantic; 19 km from Marion Island.

ROBBEN ISLAND

- Robben Island is a large island in Table Bay (5,4 km long and 2,5 km wide, with an area of 574 ha).

- It has been known to seafarers since the 15th century, and has been used for various purposes over the centuries.

- Robben Island is a Dutch name, which means 'seal island'. The island was named after the seal colonies that still live there. It was also known by the English version of the name – Seal Island – as well as Penguin Island, Robin (in French documents) and Isla de Cornelia. This name was given to the island by Joris van Spilbergen in 1601 – in honour of his mother. It was also known in Xhosa mythology as the 'Isle of Makhanda'.

- Robben Island is 11 km from Table Bay Harbour, and 7 km from Bloubergstrand.

- The treacherous rock just off the southern point of the island is called Whale Rock.

- The island has a Mediterranean climate, and an annual rainfall of between 300 and 400 mm. The highest point is 30 m above sea level.

- Over the years, the island produced seashells for Cape Town's lime kilns, and the blue slate from the island was used for buildings on the mainland.

- Visitors can see a wide variety of seabirds and marine mammals on their way to the island, such as Cape Fur seals, Southern Right whales and Dusky and Heaviside dolphins.

- The island houses 23 species of mammals, such as springbok, bontebok, European fallow deer, steenbok and eland, while reptiles such as lizards, geckoes, snakes and tortoises can also be observed. There are even a few ostriches.
- Robben Island is also home to 132 bird species, some endangered. Birds such as the Crowned cormorant and Black-crowned night herons, as well as the African penguin, use the island for breeding purposes.
- The two boats that take tourists and visitors to the island are named *Autshumato* and *Makana*. Autshumato was a Khoi leader in the 17th century. Makana (also called Nxele or Links, meaning 'left-handed') was a Xhosa warrior prophet, who became a strong advocate for the Xhosa traditions among the Ndlambe. He was banned to the island after an attack on Grahamstown, and died while trying to escape.

Year	Event
2004	Heinz Fricke, conductor of the Washington Opera, conducts the Cape Philharmonic Orchestra and the Cape Town Opera chorus at the performance of Beethoven's only opera, *Fidelio*, on 27 March.
2001	Janine Horsley, 12 years old, becomes the youngest woman to swim from Robben Island to Bloubergstrand.
2001	The Nelson Mandela Gateway in the V&A Waterfront is opened on 1 December by the former president.
1999	In December, Robben Island becomes South Africa's first World Heritage Site, together with Sterkfontein and St Lucia.
1997	Robben Island Museum is opened to the public on 1 January 1997.
1995	On 21 December, President Mandela declares Robben Island, and one nautical mile around it, a National Historical Monument.
1995	Colonel Elsa Jones is appointed both as first woman commander and last commander of Robben Island.
1991	The last political prisoners are removed from Robben Island in May.
1964	The Rivonia group is moved into the isolation section of the new prison (known as Khulukudu) when they arrive in June 1964.
1963	The lighthouse on Minto Hill is built. It is 18 m high, and has a light capacity of 464 000 candle power. It can be seen from a distance of 24 nautical miles.
1962	More than 3 000 political prisoners are held on Robben Island between 1962 and 1991. They belong to various organisations, such as the ANC, PAC, NUM, NLF, SACP, APDUSA, Liberal Party, SWAPO (Namibia), BPC, AZAPO and the UDF.
1961	The island is declared a maximum-security prison for the detention of political prisoners.
1960	Robben Island is taken over by the Correctional Services Department.
1941	Because of the fear of an attack by the Japanese, all civilians are taken from the island.
1936	The Minister of Defence, Oswald Pirow, declares Robben Island a military area.
1931	All lepers are relocated to other leper institutions. All leper buildings, except the Church of the Good Shepherd, are destroyed.
1925	A modern foghorn, the second biggest in the world, is installed on the island.
1909	Charteris Hooper becomes the first person to swim from Robben Island to Bloubergstrand.

Year	Event
1890	All women paupers who were kept on the island are transferred to Grahamstown.
1886	The first newspaper, the *Robben Island Times*, is printed.
1870	The Robben Island Primary School is built. It is used as a clubhouse in World War II.
1864	The first solid lighthouse is built on Minto Hill.
1846	Lepers, the mentally handicapped and exiles are transferred from the mainland to Robben Island.
1840	A whale factory is built on the island, but is closed when prisoners use the boats to escape.
1806	Lt Gen Sir David Baird acts as governor. The Scot, John Murray, establishes a whaling station on the island. Murray's Bay, the harbour on the island, is named after him. The other bay is known as Tangatina.
1740	The kramat next to the prison commemorates Sheikh Madura, one of the founders of Islam in South Africa. He was banned to Robben Island in the 1740s and died there.
1665	Pieter van Meerhof is appointed as commander of Robben Island. His wife, Eva Krotoa, who acted as translator in Autshumato's absence, goes with him.
1660	On 24 September 1660, Jan van Riebeeck writes to Otto Jansz on Robben Island, asking him to see to it that the 'fire beacons' are kept in good order.
1659	The first 'vuyrbaecken' [fire beacon] is lit on the island on New Year's Day.
1658	The interpreter Autshumato (or Harry) becomes the first political prisoner on the island. He also becomes the island's first escapee.
1620	Two ships anchored near Robben Island report an earthquake – the first record of this natural phenomenon in South Africa.
1614	Convicts are brought from England. Under the supervision of John Cross, they are transferred from the mainland to the island.
1601	The first sheep are taken to the island for fattening.
1488	Jao del Infante, one of Bartholomeus Dias' captains, makes a number of trips to the island.

NELSON MANDELA

- Nelson Mandela was born on 18 July 1918 at Mvezo, a village on the Mbashe River in the district of Umtata. His father was Gadla Henry Mphakanyiswa, the son of Mandela of the Ixhiba house, a house of the Madiba clan of the Thembu, who was confirmed as chief of Mvezo by the king of the Thembu tribe.

- When the little Mandela was born in 1918, his father named him Rolihlahla, a Xhosa word which literally means 'pulling the branch off a tree'. Its colloquial meaning would be 'troublemaker.' When his father lost his title because of a dispute with a magistrate, Rolihlahla and his mother moved to Qunu, which was slightly larger than Mvezo.

- On his first day of school, his teacher, Miss Mdingane, gave each of the children an English name. Rolihlahla's name was to be Nelson.

- Nelson Mandela matriculated at Healdtown Methodist Boarding School, the Wesleyan college in Fort Beaufort. He went to Fort Hare for his BA degree, but as an SRC member he participated in a student strike in 1940 and was expelled. He completed his degree by correspondence from Johannesburg, and after doing his articles of clerkship, he enrolled for an LLB at the University of the Witwatersrand.

- His daughter, Makaziwe, was born in 1947, but she died at the age of nine months. He had five other children – Madiba, Makgatho, Makaziwe, Zenani and Zindzi.

- He was married to Evelyn Mase and Winnie Madikizela before he married Graça Machel, the widow of Mozambique's president Samora Machel. She is the only woman who has been married to the heads of state of two different countries.

- Nelson Mandela was one of the founding members of the ANC Youth League in 1944, and became its secretary in 1948, and president in 1950. In 1952 he was elected as Transvaal president of the ANC and deputy national president of the ANC, and in 1991 he was elected as ANC president.

- In 1952 Nelson Mandela and Oliver Tambo opened the first black legal firm in the country.

- Nelson Mandela was tried at the Rivonia Trial in 1963, and on 12 June 1964 he was convicted of conspiracy to overthrow the government, and sentenced to life imprisonment, together with eight others. He was held at Robben Island until April 1982, when he was transferred to Pollsmoor Prison in Cape Town. In 1988, he was diagnosed as having tuberculosis, and spent several months receiving treatment at the Constantiaberg Medi-Clinic. After his release from the clinic, he was sent to Victor Verster Prison in Paarl, where he lived in house arrest at one of the warder's homes. He was released on 11 February 1990, after serving a total of 27 years.

- He was inaugurated as the first democratically elected president of the Republic of South Africa on 10 May 1994, and served in this post until June 1999, when Thabo Mbeki succeeded him.

- Nelson Mandela was chosen as *Time* magazine's 'Man of the Year' in 1993, and shared the front page with FW de Klerk, Yitzhak Rabin and Yasser Arafat.

- Nelson Rolihlahla Mandela has honorary degrees from more than 50 universities all over the world.

- A Nelson Mandela Monument was erected in Mvezo. Just across the river from the monument is Idutywa, the hometown of President Thabo Mbeki and his father, Govan.

- Mvezo also houses part of the three-part Nelson Mandela Museum. The other two parts of the museum are in Umtata and Qunu.

SOUTH AFRICA'S LEADERS SINCE 1910

	Prime minister	Political party	Age	Period(s) in office	Years in office
	Prime ministers				
1	Louis Botha	South African Party	48	1910–1919	9
2	Jan Christiaan Smuts	South African Party	49	1919–1924	5
3	James Barry Munnik (JBM) Hertzog	National Party	58	1924–1939	15
4	Jan Christiaan Smuts	United Party	69	1939–1948	9
5	Daniel Francois (DF) Malan	National Party	74	1948–1954	6
6	Johannes Gerhardus (JG) Strijdom	National Party	61	1954–1958	4
7	Hendrik Frensch (HF) Verwoerd	National Party	57	1958–1966	8
8	Balthazar Johannes (BJ) Vorster	National Party	51	1966–1978	12
9	Pieter Willem (PW) Botha	National Party	62	1978–1984	6

	Presidents	Political party	Age	Period(s) in office	Years in office
	(State) Presidents				
1	Charles Robberts (Blackie) Swart	National Party	66	1961–1968	7
2	Jacobus Johannes (Jim) Fouché	National Party	70	1968–1975	7
3	Nicolaas (Nic) Diederichs	National Party	72	1975–1978	3
4	Balthazar Johannes (BJ) Vorster	National Party	63	1978–1979	3
5	Marais Viljoen	National Party	64	1979–1984	3
6	Pieter Willem (PW) Botha	National Party	68	1984–1989	5
7	Frederik Willem (FW) de Klerk	National Party	53	1989–1994	5
8	Nelson Rolihlahla Mandela	ANC	76	1994–1999	5
9	Thabo Mvuyelwa Mbeki	ANC	57	1999–	–

Did you know?

- CR Swart, the Republic of South Africa's first state president, went to the USA in 1921 to study journalism. While he was there, he played minor roles in a few films to earn some extra money.
- Nelson Mandela has played himself in 25 films since 1991. He also played the role of a Soweto teacher in Spike Lee's *Malcolm X* (1992).
- JG Strijdom's first wife was an actress, Marda Vanne (whose real name was Margaretha 'Scrappy' van Hulsteyn). She was the daughter of Sir Willem and Lady van Hulsteyn.
- Louis Botha and JG Strijdom both died while still in office. While serving as prime minister, Hendrik Verwoerd was assassinated by Dmitri Tsafendas, a parliamentary messenger.
- South Africa's second prime minister, Jan Christiaan Smuts, did not attend

school until he was 12 years old. When he left school five years later, he was top of his class.

- Jan Smuts served as prime minister of South Africa for two terms. Five years after completing his first term, he again became prime minister when General Hertzog was forced to resign for refusing to comply with parliament's decision to take part in World War II.
- South Africa's heads of government were prime ministers until 1984, when PW Botha became the first executive state president.
- The state presidents from 1961 to 1984 were heads of state with no executive powers.
- The term 'state president' was changed to 'president' in 1994.

———————— LEADERS OF THE ————————
AFRICAN NATIONAL CONGRESS

Secretaries General of the ANC

Term	Name
1912–1917	Sol T Plaatje
1917–1919	HL Bud Mbelle
1919–1923	S Msane
1923–1927	TD Mweli Skota
1927–1930	EJ Khaile
1930–1936	Rev E Mdolomba
1936–1949	Rev J Calata
1949–1955	Walter Sisulu
1955–1958	Oliver R Tambo
1958–1969	D Nokwe
1969–1991	Alfred Nzo
1991–1997	Cyril Ramaphosa
1997–	Kgalema Motlanthe

Presidents of the ANC

Term	Name
1912–1917	Dr JL Dube
1917–1924	SM Makgatho
1924–1927	ZR Mahabane
1927–1930	JT Gumede
1930–1936	Dr Pixley ka Isaka Seme
1937–1940	ZR Mahabane
1940–1949	Dr AB Xuma
1949–1952	Dr JS Moroka
1952–1967	Chief AJ Luthuli
1967–1991	OR Tambo
1991–1997	NR Mandela
1997–	TM Mbeki

> 'We are one people. These divisions, these jealousies, are the cause of all our woes today.'   – DR PIXLEY KA ISAKA SEME (1911),
> a later president of the ANC, calling on Africans to forget the
> differences of the past and unite together in one national organisation.
> He initiated the meeting during which the ANC was founded.

Did you know?

- Various chiefs, representatives of people's and church organisations, and other prominent individuals founded the ANC on 8 January 1912.
- The delegates at the congress sang Tiyo Soga's hymn 'Lizalise Dingalako Tixo We Nyaniso' ['Fulfil thy promise, God of truth'] at the first meeting.
- The name chosen by the congress was the South African Native National Congress.
- The first ANC president, Reverend John Langalibalele Dube of Inanda, Natal, was elected in absentia. He was a cousin of Dr Pixley ka Isaka Seme.
- This first National Executive of the ANC consisted of four ministers of religion, lawyers, an editor, a building contractor, a teacher, an estate agent and an interpreter.

GENERAL ELECTION RESULTS SINCE 1994

14 April 2004
National Assembly

Registered voters	20 674 926	
Votes	15 863 554	76,7%
Invalid (spoilt) votes	250 887	1,6%
Valid votes	15 612 667	98,4%

Party	Abbr.	Votes	%	Seats
African National Congress	ANC	10 878 251	69,7	279
Democratic Alliance	DA	1 931 201	12,4	50
Inkatha Freedom Party	IFP	1 088 664	7,0	28
United Democratic Movement	UDM	355 717	2,3	9
Independent Democrats	ID	269 765	1,7	7
New National Party	NNP	257 824	1,7	7
African Christian Democratic Party	ACDP	250 272	1,6	6
Freedom Front Plus	FF Plus	139 465	0,9	4
United Christian Democratic Party	UCDP	117 792	0,8	3
Pan Africanist Congress of Azania	PAC	113 512	0,7	3
Minority Front	MF	55 267	0,4	2
Azanian People's Organisation	AZAPO	41 776	0,3	2

14 April 2004
Provincial legislatures

Registered voters	20 674 926	
Votes	15 516 223	75,0%
Invalid (spoilt) votes	213 081	1,4%
Valid votes	15 303 142	98,6%

Party	Abbr.	Votes	%	Seats
African National Congress	ANC	10 591 064	69,2	304
Democratic Alliance	DA	1 846 540	12,1	51
Inkatha Freedom Party	IFP	1 119 530	7,3	32
United Democratic Movement	UDM	349 504	2,3	10
African Christian Democratic Party	ACDP	242 924	1,6	8
New National Party	NNP	275 185	1,8	7
Independent Democrats	ID	245 277	1,6	6
Freedom Front Plus	FF Plus	139 282	0,9	5
United Christian Democratic Party	UCDP	143 515	0,9	3
Pan Africanist Congress of Azania	PAC	110 205	0,7	2
Minority Front	MF	71 540	0,5	2

Did you know?

- In the 2004 elections, voters cast their ballots at about 17 000 voting stations around the country, which opened at 7 am and closed at 9 am.
- The minimum threshold for a party to win a seat in parliament is 1%.
- A total of 21 parties took part in the election for the National Assembly, and 33 ran for the provincial parliaments.
- About 27 170 prisoners in 235 jails countrywide registered to vote.
- The Independent Electoral Commission (IEC) received notices from 1 681 South Africans who would be out of the country on voting day and wanted to vote abroad.
- The IEC used 215 412 staffers to help with the elections.
- A total of 76% of the electoral staff who were recruited were unemployed, 690 were disabled and 64% were women. A total of 274 were over 70 years old.

2 June 1999
National Assembly
Valid votes   15 977 142

Party	Abbr.	Votes	%	Seats
African National Congress	ANC	10 601 330	66,4	266
Democratic Party	DP	1 527 337	9,6	38
Inkatha Freedom Party	IFP	1 371 477	8,6	34
New National Party	NNP	1 098 215	6,9	28
United Democratic Movement	UDM	546 790	3,4	14
African Christian Democratic Party	ACDP	228 975	1,4	6
Freedom Front	FF	127 217	0,8	3
United Christian Democratic Party	UCDP	125 280	0,8	3
Pan Africanist Congress of Azania	PAC	113 125	0,7	3
Federal Alliance	FA	86 704	0,5	2
Minority Front	MF	48 277	0,3	1
Afrikaner Eenheidsbeweging	AEB	46 292	0,3	1
Azanian People's Organisation	AZAPO	27 257	0,2	1

2 June 1999
Provincial legislatures
Valid votes   15 903 753

Party	Abbr.	Votes	%	Seats
African National Congress	ANC	10 473 175	65,9	289
New National Party	NNP	1 141 362	7,2	38
Inkatha Freedom Party	IFP	1 415 541	8,9	37
Democratic Party	DP	1 416 352	8,9	35
United Democratic Movement	UDM	535 930	3,4	14
Freedom Front	FF	142 538	0,9	5
African Christian Democratic Party	ACDP	219 471	1,4	4
United Christian Democratic Party	UCDP	144 612	0,9	3
Pan Africanist Congress of Azania	PAC	121 920	0,8	2
Minority Front	MF	86 770	0,5	2
Federal Alliance	FA	82 058	0,5	1

26–29 April 1994
National Assembly

Voters	19 726 610	
Invalid (spoilt) ballots	193 112	1,0%
Valid votes	19 533 498	99,0%

Party	Abbr.	Votes	%	Seats
African National Congress	ANC	12 237 655	62,6	252
National Party	NP	3 983 690	20,4	82
Inkatha Freedom Party	IFP	2 058 294	10,5	43
Freedom Front	FF	424 555	2,2	9
Democratic Party	DP	338 426	1,7	7
Pan Africanist Congress of Azania	PAC	243 478	1,2	5
African Christian Democratic Party	ACDP	88 104	0,5	2

26–29 April 1994
Provincial legislatures

Voters	19 633 571	
Invalid (spoilt) ballots	147 841	0,8%
Valid votes	19 485 730	99,2%

Party	Abbr.	Votes	%	Seats
African National Congress	ANC	12 137 307	62,3	266
National Party	NP	3 492 467	17,9	82
Inkatha Freedom Party	IFP	2 047 083	10,5	44
Freedom Front	FF	639 643	3,3	14
Democratic Party	DP	538 655	2,8	12
Pan Africanist Congress of Azania	PAC	271 793	1,4	3
African Christian Democratic Party	ACDP	117 825	0,6	3
Minority Front	MF	48 951	0,3	1

SOME INTERESTING PARTY NAMES

Party	Abbr.	Year	National/Provincial
The Organisation Party	TOP	2004	National
Keep it Straight and Simple Party	KISS	2004	National
Green Party of South Africa	GPGP	2004	Provincial
Royal Loyal Progress	RLP	2004	Provincial
Pro-Death Penalty Party	PRO-D	2004	Provincial
Universal Party	UP	2004	Provincial
Abolition of Income Tax and Usury Party	AITUP	1999	National
The Government by the People Green Party	GPGP	1999	National
Sport Organisation for Collective Contributions and Equal Rights	SOCCER	1994	National

Party	Abbr.	Year	National/Provincial
Workers International to Rebuild the Fourth International (SA)	WI	1994	Provincial
Green Party	GRP	1994	Provincial
Merit Party	MP	1994	Provincial
Right Party	RP	1994	Provincial

SOUTH AFRICAN
GENERAL ELECTIONS SINCE 1910

Governing party and opposition					
Year	Government party	Abbr.	Seats	Opposition	Seats
1910	South African Party	SAP	66	Unionist Party	36
1915	South African Party	SAP	54	Unionist Party	40
1920	South African Party and Unionist Party (Coalition)	SAP/UP	41 25	National Party	44
1921	South African Party	SAP	79	National Party	45
1924	National Party	NP	63	South African Party	52
1929	National Party	NP	77	South African Party	61
1933	National Party Coalition	NP	75	South African Party Coalition	61
1938	United Party	UP	111	National Party	27
1943	United Party	UP	89	National Party	43
1948	National Party	NP	70	United Party	65
1953	National Party	NP	89	United Party	57
1958	National Party	NP	97	United Party	53
1961	National Party	NP	99	United Party	49
1966	National Party	NP	120	United Party	39
1970	National Party	NP	111	United Party	47
1974	National Party	NP	117	United Party	41
1977	National Party	NP	132	Progressive Federal Party	15
1981	National Party	NP	131	Progressive Federal Party	26
1987	National Party	NP	123	Conservative Party	22
1994	African National Congress	ANC	252	National Party	82
1999	African National Congress	ANC	266	Democratic Party	38
2004	African National Congress	ANC	279	Democratic Alliance	50

PROVINCES AND THEIR PREMIERS

Province	Premiers	No.	From	To
Northern Cape	Manne Dipico	1	7 May 1994	25 April 2004
	Dipuo Peters	2	26 April 2004	–
Eastern Cape	Raymond Mhlaba	1	7 May 1994	4 February 1997
	Makhenkesi Stofile	2	4 February 1997	25 April 2004
	Nosimo Balindlela	3	26 April 2004	–
Free State	Mosiuoa Patrick Lekota	1	7 May 1994	18 December 1996
	Ivy Matsepe-Casaburri	2	18 December 1996	15 June 1999
	Isabella Winkie Direko	3	15 June 1999	25 April 2004
	Beatrice Marshoff	4	26 April 2004	–
Western Cape	Hernus Kriel	1	7 May 1994	11 May 1998
	Gerald Morkel	2	11 May 1998	12 November 2001
	Cecil Herandien (acting)	–	12 November 2001	5 December 2001
	Peter Marais	3	5 December 2001	3 June 2002
	Piet Meyer (acting)	–	3 June 2002	21 June 2002
	Marthinus van Schalkwyk	4	21 June 2002	25 April 2004
	Ebrahim Rasool	5	26 April 2004	–
Limpopo	Ngoako Ramatlodi	1	7 May 1994	25 April 2004
	Sello Moloto	2	26 April 2004	–
North West	Popo Molefe	1	7 May 1994	25 April 2004
	Edna Molewa	2	26 April 2004	–
KwaZulu-Natal	Frank Mdlalose	1	11 May 1994	1 March 1997
	Ben Ngubane	2	1 March 1997	10 February 1999
	Lionel Mtshali	3	10 February 1999	25 April 2004
	S'bu Ndebele	4	26 April 2004	–
Mpumalanga	Mathews Phosa	1	7 May 1994	15 June 1999
	Ndaweni Mahlangu	2	15 June 1999	25 April 2004
	Thabang Makwetla	3	26 April 2004	–
Gauteng	Tokyo Sexwale	1	7 May 1994	19 January 1998
	Mathole Motshekga	2	19 January 1998	15 June 1999
	Mbhazima Shilowa	3	15 June 1999	25 April 2004

Did you know?

- South Africa has had a total of 28 provincial premiers in the 10 years since the first democratic elections.
- The Western Cape has had five premiers in this time, while the Northern Cape, North West and Limpopo employed only two premiers each.
- Ivy Matsepe-Casaburri was the first woman to become a premier of a South African province, when she headed the Free State. Two other women premiers succeeded her – Isabella Winkie Direko and Beatrice Marshoff.
- When South Africa's first nine provincial premiers were elected in 1994, there

were no women. In 2004, four provinces had women as premiers: Free State, Eastern Cape, Northern Cape and North West.

SPEAKERS OF THE SOUTH AFRICAN PARLIAMENT SINCE 1910

Speaker	From	To
Sir James Molteno	1 November 1910	18 November 1915
CJ Krige	19 November 1915	24 July 1924
Dr EG Jansen	25 July 1915	19 July 1929
JHH de Waal	19 July 1929	25 May 1933
Dr EG Jansen	26 May 1933	21 January 1944
CM van Coller	22 January 1944	5 August 1948
JF Naudé	6 August 1948	7 November 1950
JH Conradie	19 January 1951	31 December 1960
HJ Klopper	20 January 1961	1 August 1974
AJ Schlebusch	2 August 1974	25 January 1976
JJ Loots	26 January 1976	30 July 1981
JP du Toit	31 July 1981	13 February 1983
JW Greeff	14 February 1983	1 January 1987
L le Grange	2 January 1987	26 October 1991
E van der M Louw	14 October 1991	26 April 1994
Dr Frene Ginwala	27 April 1994	02 April 2004
Baleka Mbete	3 May 2004	–

Did you know?

• Dr Frene Ginwala was the first woman to become Speaker of the South African parliament. She was elected to this post in 1994, and was succeeded by another woman, Ms Baleka Mbete, in 2004.

• In June 2002, Frene Ginwala and Naledi Pandor, Chairperson of the National Council of Provinces, were two of only 25 women around the world to preside over a house of the 1 809 parliaments. South Africa was one of only three African countries to have women presiding officers in parliament or a house of parliament.

WOMEN IN THE CABINET: 2004

• In April 2004, President Thabo Mbeki appointed three more women into his cabinet. He also retained nine women cabinet ministers and promoted three deputy ministers – the highest representation of women in cabinet that South Africa – or Africa – has ever seen.

• The 2004 cabinet has 16 men and 12 women, while there are 11 men and 10 women among the deputy ministers.

• 43% of South Africa's cabinet ministers are women, up from 30% in 1999.

Ministers	Portfolio
Thoko Didiza	Agriculture and Land Affairs
Ivy Matsepe-Casaburri	Communications
Naledi Pandor	Education
Nkosazana Dlamini-Zuma	Foreign Affairs
Mantombazana Tshabalala-Msimang	Health
Nosiviwe Mapisa-Nqakula	Home Affairs
Lindiwe Sisulu	Housing
Bridgette Mabandla	Justice and Constitutional Development
Phumzile Mlambo-Ngcuka	Minerals and Energy
Geraldine Fraser-Moleketi	Public Service and Administration
Stella Sigcau	Public Works
Buyelwa Sonjica	Water Affairs and Forestry

Deputy ministers	Portfolio
Ntombazana Botha	Arts and Culture
Cheryl Gillwald	Correctional Services
Rejoice Mabudafhasi	Environmental Affairs and Tourism
Sue van der Merwe	Foreign Affairs
Nosizwe Madlala-Routledge	Health
Lulu Xingwana	Minerals and Energy
Nomatyala Hangana	Provincial and Local Government
Susan Shabangu	Safety and Security
Jean Benjamin	Social Development
Lindiwe Hendricks	Trade and Industry

Did you know?

- 30% of all South African parliamentarians are women, which puts South Africa at number eight in the world in terms of gender equality in government, which is quite a leap from the 141st position it held before the 1994 elections.
- South Africa has the world's third highest proportion of companies employing women as senior managers. According to the annual Grant Thornton International Business Owners Survey, 75% of South African businesses employ women in senior management positions. The world average is 59%.
- In South Africa, women fill 26% of senior management posts, compared to the global average of 7%. This gives South Africa the eighth place in the world.
- Russia has the highest proportion (89%) of companies where women occupy a management role, followed by the Philippines (85%), while the United States and Mexico are on the same level as South Africa (75%). The Netherlands and Pakistan (27%), Japan (29%) and Germany (33%) bring up the rear.
- In Russia, the only country close to full gender parity, women hold 42% of management posts. Although the USA has women in senior management positions, in 75% of its businesses, women have only 20% of the senior jobs.

TRADITIONAL LEADERS
IN SOUTH AFRICA

- According to the *Draft White Paper on Traditional Leadership and Governance* (October 2002), issued by the Department of Provincial and Local Government, the following traditional leaders are remunerated by government:

Province	Kings/Queens	Chiefs	Headmen
Eastern Cape	6	173	935
North West	0	68	100
Limpopo	1	188	527
Mpumalanga	2	51	0
KwaZulu-Natal	1	280	0
Free State	2	13	78
Western Cape	0	0	0
Northern Cape	0	0	0
Gauteng	0	0	0
Total	**12**	**773**	**1 640**

Did you know?

During colonial times, the term 'king' was never used to refer to traditional rulers, as it was reserved only for the king of England.

ZULU KINGS

- The Zulus are a Nguni group that established itself in southern Africa in the 17th century. It was originally a relatively unimportant tribe, until Shaka became king in 1816. He revolutionised Zulu warfare and established a strong empire.
- Senzangakhona sent his son, Shaka, away from the tribe. Shaka found refuge with King Dingiswayo of the neighbouring Mthethwa tribe, and when Shaka's father died, Dingiswayo nominated Shaka as Zulu king. Shaka created a Zulu empire that surpassed anything his father or the neighbouring tribes had envisaged.
- King Cetshwayo became famous for the victory that his forces achieved against British troops at Isandhlwana (as depicted in the film *Zulu Dawn*). A second battle at Rorke's Drift was not so successful (as seen in the film *Zulu*).

King		Father	Reigned
Malandela		Luzumana	–
Ntombhela	–	Malandela	–
Zulu	–	Ntombhela	–
Ghumede	–	Zulu	–
Phunga	–	Ghumede	Until 1727
Mageba	† 1745	Phunga	1727–1745
Ndaba	† 1763	Mageba	1745–1763
Jama	† 1781	Ndaba	1763–1781
Senzangakhona	ca. 1762–1816	Jama	1781–1816
Shaka	ca. 1787–1828	Senzangakhona	1816–1828
Dingane	ca. 1795–1840	Senzangakhona	1828–1840
Mpande	1798–1872	Senzangakhona	1840–1872
Cetshwayo	1826–February 1884	Mpande	1872–1884
Dinizulu	1868–1913	Cetshwayo	1884–1913
Solomon	1891–1933	Dinizulu	1913–1933
Cyprian Bhekuzulu	4 August 1924–17 September 1968	Solomon	1933–1968
Goodwill Zwelethini	born 14 July 1948	Cyprian	1968

Did you know?

In the Zulu language, *zulu* means 'heaven' or 'sky'.

THE CONSTITUTION OF THE REPUBLIC OF SOUTH AFRICA

As adopted on 8 May 1996 and amended on 11 October 1996 by the Constitutional Assembly.

One law for One nation

∾ PREAMBLE ∾

We, the people of South Africa,

Recognise the injustices of our past;

Honour those who suffered for justice and freedom in our land;

Respect those who have worked to build and develop our country; and

Believe that South Africa belongs to all who live in it, united in our diversity.

We therefore, through our freely elected representatives, adopt this Constitution as the supreme law of the Republic so as to –

Heal the divisions of the past and establish a society based on democratic values, social justice and fundamental human rights;

Lay the foundations for a democratic and open society in which government is based on the will of the people and every citizen is equally protected by law;

Improve the quality of life of all citizens and free the potential of each person; and
Build a united and democratic South Africa able to take its rightful place as a sovereign state in the family of nations.

May God protect our people.

Nkosi Sikelel' iAfrika. Morena boloka setjhaba sa heso.

God seën Suid-Afrika. God bless South Africa.

Mudzimu fhaṱutshedza Afurika. Hosi katekisa Afrika.

Constitution of the Republic of South Africa

Chapters	Content
Chapter 1	Founding Provisions
Chapter 2	Bill of Rights
Chapter 3	Co-operative Government
Chapter 4	Parliament
Chapter 5	The President and National Executive
Chapter 6	Provinces
Chapter 7	Local Government
Chapter 8	Courts and Administration of Justice
Chapter 9	State Institutions Supporting Constitutional Democracy
Chapter 10	Public Administration
Chapter 11	Security Services
Chapter 12	Traditional Leaders
Chapter 13	Finance
Chapter 14	General Provisions

Schedules	Content
Schedule 1	National Flag
Schedule 2	Oaths and Solemn Affirmations
Schedule 3	Election Procedures
Schedule 4	Functional Areas of Concurrent National and Provincial Legislative Competence
Schedule 5	Functional Areas of Exclusive Provincial Legislative Competence
Schedule 6	Transitional Arrangements
Schedule 7	Laws Repealed

MINISTERS OF FOREIGN AFFAIRS

Period	Minister of Foreign Affairs
1927–1955	The prime minister
1955–1964	Eric Louw
1964–1977	Hilgard Muller
1977–1994	Roelof Frederik (Pik) Botha
1994–1999	Alfred Nzo
1999–2004	Nkosazana Dlamini-Zuma
2004–	Nkosazana Dlamini-Zuma

MINISTERS OF FINANCE

Period	Minister of Finance
1910–1912	HC Hull
1912–1915	Gen. JC Smuts
1915–1917	Sir DP de V Graaff
1917–1920	T Orr
1920–1924	H Burton
1924–1939	NC Havenga
1939–1948	JH Hofmeyr
1948–1954	NC Havenga
1954–1958	EH Louw
1958–1961	JF Naudé
1961–1968	TE Dönges
1968–1975	N Diederichs
1975–1984	O Horwood
1984–1992	Barend du Plessis
1992–1995	Derek Keys
1995–1996	Chris Liebenberg
1996–	Trevor Manuel

THE SOUTH AFRICAN RESERVE BANK

- The South African Reserve Bank, the central bank of the Republic of South Africa, was established in 1921 in terms of a special Act of parliament, the Currency and Bank Act of 10 August 1920. It opened its doors for business for the first time on 30 June 1921.
- The South African Reserve Bank was only the fourth central bank established outside Britain and Europe. The other three were in the USA, Japan and Java. England has the world's oldest central bank. It was founded in 1694.
- Tito Mboweni is the seventh governor of the South African Reserve Bank. His predecessors were:

WH Clegg	1920–1931
J Postmus	1932–1945
MH de Kock	1945–1962
G Rissik	1962–1967
TW de Jongh	1967–1980
GPC de Kock	1981–1989
C Stals	1989–1999

- Dr MH de Kock's signature was the first to appear on rand notes, after decimalisation in 1961.

- Dr GPC de Kock (governor from 1981 to 1989) was the son of Dr MH de Kock (governor from 1945 to 1962).
- Gill Marcus was the first woman to be appointed as deputy governor of the South African Reserve Bank.
- The Afrikaans title for the governor of the Reserve Bank is 'president'.
- The Reserve Bank has always been privately owned, and it has about 650 shareholders. No individual shareholder may hold more than 10 000 shares out of the total of 2 000 000 issued shares.
- The Reserve Bank has a board of 14 directors, which includes the governor and three deputy governors, who are all appointed by the government for five-year terms.
- The government appoints three other directors for a period of three years, and shareholders elect the seven other directors (one representing agriculture, two industry, and four commerce or finance) for a period of three years.
- The Reserve Bank's repo rate influences the interest rates charged by banks, the general level of interest rates in the economy, and therefore other economic aggregates such as money supply, bank credit extension and, ultimately, the rate of inflation.

THE REPO RATE

- The repo rate has played a large role in South Africans' lives over the past few years, and home owners tend to watch its ebb and flow like hawks, because the Reserve Bank can indirectly influence the cost at which money is made available to commercial banks through the daily refinancing of the banks' cash requirement.
- The daily refinancing of the banks occurs by way of a weekly tender, and if they tender successfully, the banks sell financial assets to the Reserve Bank in exchange for cash.
- This tendering system, which was introduced in March 1998, is called the 'repurchase' or 'repo' system. The commercial banks sell assets to the Reserve Bank, but have to buy back (repurchase) the assets after an agreed period (normally seven days). This is why the system is called the 'repo' system.
- Banks enter into repo transactions (selling with an obligation to repurchase) with the Reserve Bank when they have a need for cash.
- The average rate at which all the banks tender for the cash that the Reserve Bank provides is called the repo rate.

- It is currently a variable rate, which is partly determined by the banks, depending on their tenders.
- Whenever necessary, the Reserve Bank may fix the repo rate, for example because of the uncertainty at the time of the millennium date changeover (1999 to 2000).

Changes in South Africa's repo rate since 1999

Repo rate	Date
12	25 November 1999
11,75	14 January 2001
12	17 October 2000
11	15 June 2001
10	05 September 2001
9,5	21 September 2001
10,5	16 January 2002
11,5	15 March 2002
12,5	14 June 2002
13,5	13 September 2002
12	13 June 2002
11	15 August 2003
10	11 September 2003
8,5	17 October 2003
8	12 December 2003
7,5	12 August 2004

BANKNOTES

The Big Five are depicted on the South African banknotes:

Value	Year	Colour	Obverse	Reverse	Representing	Issued	Dimensions	Designer
R10	1993	Green	Rhinoceros	Sheep	Agriculture	1 October 1993	70 x 128 mm	Ernst de Jong
R20	1999	Brown	Elephants	Mining	Mining	1 April 1993	70 x 134 mm	Ernst de Jong
R50	1992	Red	Lions	Oil refinery	Manufacturing	1 October 1992	70 x 140 mm	Ernst de Jong
R100	1994	Purple-blue	Cape buffalo	Zebras	Tourism	2 April 1994	70 x 146 mm	Ernst de Jong
R200	1994	Orange	Leopard	Bridge, antenna	Transport and Communications	1 October 1994	70 x 152 mm	Ernst de Jong

Did you know?
- The governor of the Cape, Joachim van Plettenberg, first introduced paper money in the Cape in 1782, because he could not get enough coins from Holland for the requirements of the settlement. This paper money was issued in rixdollar and stiver denominations, which was the Cape currency at the time.
- There was no printing press in the Cape, and the notes had to be hand-written

until about 1803. A government fiscal hand-stamp indicated the value and date of the issue. After 1803, all notes were printed.

- The first bank at the Cape was the Lombard Bank, a state bank that opened in 1793 to bring extra money into circulation. This bank issued the government notes, but by 1883 it was forced out of business by private banks. The first private bank, the Cape of Good Hope Bank, opened in 1837.
- The South African Bank Note Company (Pty) Ltd manufactures banknotes on behalf of the South African Reserve Bank.

THE BIG FIVE IN 11 LANGUAGES

English	Afrikaans	Sesotho	Setswana	siSwati	Tshivenda	Xitsonga
Big Five	Groot Vyf	Tse golo tse hlano	Tse kgolo tse hlano	Letinkhulu letisihlanu	Khulwane thanu	Swiharhi swa ntlhanu leswikulu
Elephant	Olifant	Tlou	Tlou	Indlovu	Ndou	Ndlopfu
Rhinoceros	Renoster	Kudu	Tshukudu	Bhejane	Tshugulu	Mhelembe
Buffalo	Buffel	Pholo	Nare	Ingongoni	Nari	Nyarhi
Lion	Leeu	Tau	Tau	Libhubesi	Ndau	Nghala
Leopard	Luiperd	Lengau	Lengau	Ingwe	Nngwe	Yingwe

English	isiZulu	isiXhosa	isiNdebele	Sepedi
Big Five	Ezinkulu ezinhlanu	Isihlanu esikhulu	Ezikulu Ezihlanu	Tse Thlano tse kgolo
Elephant	Indlovu	Indlovu	Indlovu	Tlou
Rhinoceros	Ubhejane	Umkhombe	Ifarigi yommango	Tšhukudu
Buffalo	Inyathi	Inyathi	Imbevula	Nare
Lion	Ibhubesi	Ingonyama	Ibhubezi	Tau
Leopard	Ingwe	Ihlosi	Ingwenyama	Nkwe

—— COINS ——

Coin	Image	Series	Released	Composition	Diameter	Mass
1c*	Cape sparrow	Red	Sept. 1990	Steel core plated with composition of copper	15 mm	1,50 g
2c*	Fish eagle	Red	Aug. 1991	Steel core plated with composition of copper	16 mm	2,00 g
5c	Blue crane	Red	Sept. 1990	Steel core plated with composition of copper	18 mm	3,00 g
10c	Arum lily	Yellow	Dec. 1990	Steel core plated with copper (88%) and tin	19 mm	3,50 g
20c	Protea	Yellow	May 1992	Steel core plated with copper (88%) and tin	20 mm	4,00 g
50c	Strelitzia	Yellow	May 1991	Steel core plated with copper (88%) and tin	21 mm	4,50 g
R1	Springbok	White	Nov. 1991	Copper core plated with nickel	22 mm	5,00 g
R2	Kudu	White	Nov. 1989	Copper core plated with nickel	23 mm	5,50 g
R5	Black wildebeest	White	May 1994	Copper core plated with nickel	26 mm	7,00 g
R5	Black wildebeest	White/ yellow	Aug. 2004	Bronze-coloured core, silver-coloured border	26 mm	9,50 g

* The 1c and 2c coins are not minted any more.

Did you know?

- The 1c, 2c and 5c, the red series, consists of a steel core plated with a composition of copper. The coins have smooth edges, and display birds.
- The 10c, 20c and 50c, the yellow series, consists of a steel core plated with a composition of copper and tin. The coins have serrated edges, and display wild flowers.
- The R1, R2, R5, the white series, consists of a copper core plated with nickel. The coins' edges are serrated and smooth, and display antelope species.
- On 2 August 2004 a new R5 coin was introduced, because it was too easy for counterfeiters to reproduce the old coin. The older coin will remain legal tender and will stay in circulation, together with the new coin, until it is eventually phased out of circulation.
- The new R5 coin consists of two metals. The coin has a bronze-coloured core and a silver-coloured border. It still depicts the black wildebeest on the reverse side, and the coat of arms on the obverse side. The new coin is slightly heavier and thicker than the old coin. A security groove is on the rim of the coin; serrations are on both sides of the security groove; 'SARB R5' is engraved into the security groove and there is micro-lettering depicting 'SARB' on the reverse side of the coin.
- A leopard design was originally considered for the R2 coin, but it was decided that the R1, R2 and R5 should all depict antelopes.
- The black wildebeest (on the R5) was originally used as the provincial animal emblem of the Free State and Natal.

- South Africa's currency unit, the rand, took its name from the Witwatersrand, which is known as 'The Rand'.
- The rand has been South Africa's official currency unit since 14 February 1961, when it replaced the pound. South Africa has had five coin series over the years: ZAR coins – 1892; British pounds – 1923; decimal rand and cent – 1961; decimal rand and cent second series – 1965; and the current series of electroplated coins, which has been in use since 1989.
- South Africa's first Mint was opened in 1923 in Visagie Street, Pretoria. It became South Africa's only Mint in 1941, when all ties with the British Royal Mint were severed.
- The second Mint was opened on 22 November 1978, on the same site as the first.
- A private company, the South African Mint Company (Pty) Ltd, has been producing all South Africa's coins since 1988 on behalf of the Reserve bank. The Mint moved to Gateway, an industrial suburb of Centurion near Pretoria, in 1992.

South African coins (continued)				
Value	Design	Afrikaans	Scientific	Artist
1c	Cape sparrow[1]	Mossie	*Passer melanurus*	W Lumley
2c	Fish eagle	Visarend	*Haliaetus vocifer*	A Sutherland
5c	Blue crane[2]	Bloukraanvoël	*Anthropoides paradisea*	G Richard
10c	Arum lily[3]	Aronskelk	*Zantedeschia aethiopica*	RC McFarlane
20c	King protea[4]	Reuse protea	*Protea cynaroids*	S Erasmus
50c	Strelitzia[5]	Kraanvoëlblom	*Strelitzia reginae*	L Lotriet
R1	Springbok[6]	Springbok	*Antidorcas marsupialis*	L Lotriet
R2	Kudu	Koedoe	*Tragelaphus strepsiceros*	A Sutherland
R5	Black wildebeest	Swartwildebees	*Connochaetes gnou*	A Sutherland

1 The two sparrows on a mimosa branch, drawn by Kruger Gray, was seen on the farthing (1923–1960) and on the ½ cent (1961–1964).

2 The blue crane was depicted on the nickel 5c of South Africa's second decimal series (1965–1989).

3 The arum lily, which is also known as the white calla lily, aronskelk, varkblom or pig lily, was originally used for the 50c coin (1965–1989) as part of South Africa's second decimal series.

4 The protea was first depicted on the tickey and sixpence coins (1923–1960), and on the 2½c and 5c coins of South Africa's first decimal series (1961–1964).

5 The crane flower or bird-of-paradise flower was depicted together with the arum lily and blue agapanthus on the 50c coin that was used from 1965 in the second decimal series. It is also used as the civic emblem of the American city of Los Angeles.

6 The springbok was first used in 1947 on silver crown coins. Coert Steynberg, the famous sculptor, designed the orginal springbok. Other coins with a springbok are the gold £1 and £½ coins, and the gold R1 and R2 coins. It also appeared on the reverse of the 50c (1961–1964) and on the krugerrand since 1967. It was used for the R1 nickel coins from 1977 to 1990. The words *Soli Deo Gloria* on the R1 coin mean 'To God alone the glory'.

Did you know?

- If a South African millionaire wants to keep his money in 1c coins under his bed, he would first have to install a strong floor. R1 million's 1c pieces weigh 15 000 kg!
- If the millionaire decides to take his money in R10 notes, and puts them next to each other, the money road will go on for 12,8 km. If he decides to use R200 notes, the road will be 7,6 km long.

Some bits 'n pieces

- The first Krugerrand was struck in Pretoria in 1967. The sculptor Coert Steynberg designed the springbok on this coin.
- JM Goodenough imported South Africa's first cash register on 23 September 1923 from Ohio in the USA.
- In 1977, a cheque for R77 was written on a piglet named Frank, and cashed at a Johannesburg bank by Paul Hillen.
- South Africa's first airmail postage stamps were sold in February 1925.

SA RAND/US DOLLAR EXCHANGE RATE 1971–2004

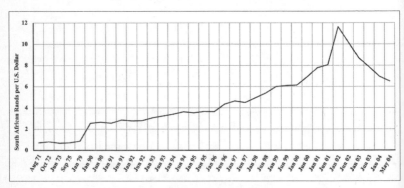

THE JSE SECURITIES EXCHANGE

- The world's oldest stock exchange was founded in the Oude Zijds Kapel in Amsterdam in 1602.
- The Johannesburg Stock Exchange is currently the only stock exchange in South Africa. When it was established in 1887, there were already two stock exchanges in Barberton, as well as exchanges in Kimberley, Cape Town, Pietermaritzburg and Durban.

- Benjamin Minors Woollan, 36, founded Johannesburg's first stock exchange in November 1887, a mere nine months after President Paul Kruger proclaimed the nine farms of the Witwatersrand goldfields as public diggings. It was orginally known as the Johannesburg Exchange & Chambers Company, and its address was '**Corner of Commissioner and Simmonds Streets**'.
- After three years the old building was too small, and was replaced by a new one, which also became too small in record time, spilling some of the trading activities onto the streets.
- When the mining commissioner closed the part of Simmonds Street between Commissioner Street and Market Square to all vehicles, the well-known and much-used phrase 'between the chains' was born. The heading for the stock exchange price in the *Star* was, 'Between the Chains'.
- The JSE's next home was a three-storey building in **Hollard Street**, covering a city block between Fox, Main, Hollard and Sauer streets.
- This building also proved to be too small, and the members accepted a resolution to build a larger home for the JSE in Hollard Street, which meant that the JSE was housed temporarily in Protection House in Fox Street. The new building was officially opened in February 1961.
- Seventeen years later, on 12 December 1978, the JSE moved to **Diagonal Street**, which became a synonym for South Africa's economic heartbeat.
- Another significant 'move' took place on Friday 7 June 1996. When the final bell rang at 4 pm for the close of trading, it also closed the trading floor for good, signalling the takeover by the latest computer technology, with all future trade to be conducted on the JSE Equities Trading system (JET).
- Four years later, in September 2000, the JSE moved yet again, this time to a modern building at the corner of Gwen Lane and Maude Street in **Sandton**, a suburb of Johannesburg.
- Die JET system was followed by Online Trading and Strate (Share Transactions Totally Electronic).
- In May 2002 the JSE began to use the electronic trading system of the London Stock Exchange, better known as SETS. This system is in London, and is linked to a mainframe in Johannesburg.

PETROL PRICE 1990–2004

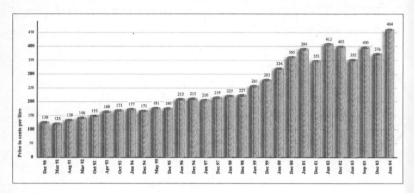

SOUTH AFRICA'S NATIONAL ROADS AND ROUTES

Did you know?

- South Africa has the longest road network of any country in Africa, a total of approximately 535 000 km, of which 105 000 km is paved.
- The South African government, represented by the Minister of Transport, is the sole shareholder and owner of the National Roads Agency, which maintains and manages the 9 600-km national road network. It has more than R40 billion in assets, excluding the land.
- The national road network includes 1 501 km of dual-carriage freeway, and 462 km of single-carriage freeway.
- At the end of 2001 there were 6,9 million registered vehicles in South Africa, of which more than 3,98 million were motor vehicles. The number of private motor vehicles grows at a rate of 1,7% per year.
- The 127 000 minibus taxis in South Africa provide 65% of the 2,5 billion annual passenger trips in urban areas, as well as a high percentage of rural transport.
- South Africa's toll roads have 33 mainline toll plazas, and cover about 2 400 km.
- Every year approximately 10 000 people are killed and 150 000 injured in more than 500 000 road-traffic accidents. The annual cost of these accidents is estimated to be more than R13 billion.
- The proclaimed national roads and the national routes in the country are numbered from N1 to N22. There is no N13 ...

National Road	From	Route followed	To
N1	Zimbabwe (Beitbridge border crossing)	Pietersburg – Potgietersrus – Pretoria – Johannesburg – Winburg – Bloemfontein – Colesberg – Hanover – Three Sisters – Beaufort West – Worcester	Cape Town
N2	Cape Town	Somerset West – Swellendam – Mossel Bay – George – Port Elizabeth – Ncanara – Grahamstown – King William's Town – East London – Umtata – Durban – Piet Retief	Ermelo
N3	Johannesburg	Harrismith – Ladysmith – Pietermaritzburg	Durban
N4	Botswana (Skilpadshek border crossing)	Pretoria – Witbank – Middelburg	Mozambique (Lebombo border crossing)
N5	Winburg	Bethlehem	Harrismith
N6	Bloemfontein	Queenstown	East London
N7	Namibia (Vioolsdrif border crossing)	Springbok	Cape Town
N8	Bloemfontein	Ladybrand	Lesotho (Maseru bridge border crossing)
N9	Colesberg	Middelburg – Graaff-Reinet	George
N10	Namibia (Nakop border crossing)	Upington – Britstown – De Aar – Hanover – Middelburg – Cradock	Ncanara
N11	Botswana (Grobler's Bridge border crossing)	Potgietersrus – Middelburg – Ermelo	Ladysmith
N12	George	Beaufort West – Three Sisters – Britstown – Kimberley – Warrenton – Klerksdorp – Potchefstroom – Johannesburg	Witbank
(N13)	–	(Formerly Johannesburg southern bypass)	–
N14	Springbok	Upington – Vryburg – Krugersdorp – Centurion	Pretoria
N17	Johannesburg	Leandra – Bethal – Ermelo	Swaziland (Oshoek border crossing)

DISTANCES IN SOUTH AFRICA (in km)

Beaufort West																	
535	Bloemfontein																
463	998	Cape Town															
316	219	779	Colesberg														
1 225	667	1 660	881	Durban													
597	575	1 042	518	667	East London												
237	764	436	545	1 240	630	George											
951	417	1 405	623	598	992	734	Johannesburg										
497	175	960	284	842	750	1 168	467	Kimberley									
1 386	854	1 886	1 058	774	1 308	1 603	465	939	Komatipoort								
273	808	392	608	1 306	696	66	1 234	770	1 669	Mossel Bay							
1 293	771	1 770	964	689	1 214	1 509	358	832	87	1 575	Nelspruit						
179	714	422	495	1 244	689	63	1 130	676	1 565	94	1 472	Oudtshoorn					
1 486	952	1 940	1 158	910	1 391	1 686	535	1 009	308	1 726	221	1 391	Phalaborwa				
405	635	756	454	927	300	330	1 062	752	1 484	396	1 373	358	1 524	Port Elizabeth			
1 009	475	1 463	681	656	1 050	1 226	58	532	429	1 292	342	1 188	477	1 120	Pretoria		
440	975	49	756	1 594	1 070	392	1 391	937	1 826	363	1 733	399	1 866	739	1 449	Stellenbosch	
1 656	1 890	1 469	1 772	2 557	2 280	1 761	2 189	1 715	2 545	1 797	2 458	1 703	2 617	2 077	2 116	1 462	Windhoek

---

SOUTH AFRICA'S TOLL PLAZAS

The toll road is here to stay. There are an amazing number of these roads on the national road network, mainly on five different routes.

N1	N2	N3	N4	N17
Huguenot	Tsitsikamma	Mariannhill	Pelindaba	Gosforth
Verkeerdevlei	Umtentweni	Tugela	Quagga	Dalpark
Vaal	Tongaat	Bergville	Middelburg	Brakpan/Denne
Grasmere	Mvoti	Mooi	Machadodorp	
Carousel	Mtunzini	Treverton	Nkomazi	
Wallmansthal	Mandini	Wilge	Doornpoort	
Murrayhill	Dokodweni	De Hoek	K99	
Hammanskraal	Oribi		Swartruggens	
Maubane	Izotsha		Brits	
Pumulani			Buffelspoort	
Zambesi			Marikana	
Stormvoël			Kroondal	
Kranskop				
Nyl				
Sebetiela				
Capricorn				
Baobab				

Did you know?
• The total cost of travelling once on *all* these toll roads would be R718,00.

MARK SHUTTLEWORTH:
FIRST AFRICAN IN SPACE

• On 25 April 2002, Mark Shuttleworth became the first South African in space, when he boarded the Soyuz spacecraft, which would take him to the International Space Station (ISS).
• Shuttleworth, a South African Internet billionaire and the world's second space tourist, was born in Welkom on 18 September 1973, and grew up in Cape Town.
• In 1995, his final year at the University of Cape Town, Shuttleworth founded Thawte Consulting, an Internet consulting business. The company's focus shifted to Internet security for electronic commerce, and it became the first company to produce a full-security e-commerce web server that was commercially available outside the United States.
• Thawte became the fastest-growing Internet Certificate Authority, and was the leading Certificate Authority outside of the US when it was acquired by VeriSign in the USA in 1999, for an amount of R3,5 billion.

- Shuttleworth received his training at Star City, and the Soyuz (like all Russian spacecraft) was launched from Baikonur, which is not in Russia, but in neighbouring Kazakhstan. That is also where the Baikonur Space Centre or Cosmodrome is, which was Shuttleworth's home during the last week before his trip.
- Mark Shuttleworth's Russian nickname for the journey was Boeranof.
- The Baikonur Cosmodrome is the world's oldest launch pad for space flight. The world's first satellite, the *Sputnik*, was launched there in 1957, and Yuri Gagarin, the first human in space, was launched from it four years later.
- The Americans call their space travellers astronauts, while the Russians call them cosmonauts. A new name was coined for Mark Shuttleworth – 'afronaut' – because he was the first African in space.
- The ISS orbits the Earth on an average altitude of almost 400 km. When Mark Shuttleworth was on the ISS as it travelled over South Africa, he was closer to his home country than he was when he was in Moscow.
- The Concorde aeroplane flew at a height of 17 km, and a Boeing flies at 12,5 km. Concorde flew at 2 400 km/h, and a Boeing flies at 640 km/h. The speed of sound is 1 233 km/h (or Mach 1). The ISS moves at a speed of 28 000 km/h.
- The construction work on the ISS, the heaviest object in orbit around the Earth after the moon, started in 1998. While the station was still being planned, President Ronald Reagan of America announced the original name, Freedom. The name was changed to International Space Station after Russia joined the project.
- The Russian Mir space station was the first permanent space station in orbit around the Earth, but it was brought back to Earth and fell into the Pacific Ocean earlier in 2002. *Mir* means 'peace'.
- America, Japan, Canada, Brazil and 11 countries that are part of the European Space Agency were involved in the development of the ISS.
- It will take another three years of space visits to the ISS before it is completed. The ISS have cabins that can house seven spacemen for up to six months at a time.
- The ISS has eight solar panels that convert rays of sunshine into electricity. It orbits the earth about 16 times a day, which means that the cosmonauts or astronauts see 16 sunsets and sunrises every day! Extra electricity is stored in batteries for use when the ISS travels in the shadow of the Earth.
- One of the things Mark Shuttleworth wanted to do with his journey to space was to make children aware that mathematics and science can be interesting. His company also launched the Hip2b^2 project to create this awareness.

- The other two crewmembers were Yuri Gidzenko (40, commander), who had spent 330 days in space aboard Mir and the ISS before the flight, and the flight engineer, Italy's Roberto Vittori, a test and fighter pilot.
- They journeyed to the ISS in a Russian-built Soyuz TM-34 capsule, which was 7,5 m long, and weighed just over 7 tons. It was launched by a Soyuz-U rocket, and took a day to reach the ISS.
- Shuttleworth conducted several scientific experiments during his 10 days in space. He did the world's first experiment to assess the impact of zero-gravity on the development of stem cells and embryos. Another experiment determined the effect of microgravity on the cardiovascular system and muscles. The third experiment was an attempt to crystallise HIV proteins in weightlessness in the hopes that, when X-rayed, they will give an accurate view of the virus structure. The experiments were managed by South African scientists from the Universities of Cape Town, Stellenbosch and Port Elizabeth, in collaboration with Russian space-science experts.

SOUTH AFRICA'S SECOND SPACE TRAVELLER

- Mike Melvill, a South African-born test pilot, made history in the rocket aeroplane *SpaceShipOne* on Monday 21 June 2004, when it became the first privately financed, manned craft to reach space.
- He earned his wings, officially, as an astronaut, to become the second South African in space after Mark Shuttleworth.
- He also became the first civilian to fly a spaceship out of the atmosphere and the first private pilot to earn astronaut wings.
- *SpaceShipOne* was carried to about 15 km, slung beneath another aeroplane, *White Knight*.
- After an hour's climbing, *SpaceShipOne* was released when the rocket fired, sending the craft to the top of its trajectory, at an altitude of 100,095 km (as confirmed by radar).
- *SpaceShipOne* and *White Knight* were both built by a team headed by aircraft designer Burt Rutan, who became famous for designing the *Voyager* aircraft, which flew non-stop and without refuelling around the world in 1986.
- Rutan set up a special company, Scaled Composites, to develop and build *SpaceShipOne*, at a cost of $20 million. Microsoft co-founder Paul Allen funded the project.

- Mike Melvill is the vice-president and general manager of Scaled Composites, LLC, and has 19 years' experience as an experimental test pilot.
- He was born in Johannesburg and raised in Durban, where he attended the nearby Hilton College. He and his wife Sally, who is from KwaZulu-Natal, were married in the United Kingdom in the mid-1960s, and they now live in Tehachapi, California.
- In 1997 he decided to fly his homebuilt aeroplane, the *Long-EZ*, to South Africa, but extended it to an around-the-world trip. He stopped in Windhoek, Cape Town, Durban and Johannesburg to visit friends and family. His trip took him nearly three months and 232 hours in the cockpit.
- At the end of June 2004, Melvill had a total flight time of 6 950 hours in 127 fixed-wing aicraft and 11 helicopters.

What he said afterwards …
'You got a hell of a view from 100 km. The flight was spectacular. Looking out that window, seeing the white clouds in the LA Basin, it looked like snow on the ground. As I got to the top I released a bag of M&Ms (sweets) in the cockpit. It was amazing.'

SUNSAT: SOUTH AFRICA'S FIRST SATELLITE

- *Sunsat* was South Africa's first satellite (actually a micro-satellite), built by post-graduate engineering students in the Department of Electrical and Electronic Engineering at the University of Stellenbosch.
- *Sunsat* was launched at the 11th attempt, on 23 February 1999, on a Delta II launch vehicle.
- Its load included NASA experiments, radio amateur communications, a high-resolution imager, precision altitude control and school experiments.
- *Sunsat* was operational for nearly two years, until late February 2001, when contact from the ground station was established for the last time.
- The project was so successful that subsystems were sold to satellite programmes in South Korea, Germany and Australia.
- This led to the creation of the spin-off company SunSpace Information Systems, which develops and manufactures satellites and satellite subsystems commercially.

Did you know?

- In 2003, the People's Republic of China became only the third country to launch a manned spacecraft, when it sent its first spaceship, *Shenzhou*, into space. (*Shenzhou* means 'divine ship').

- Americans call their space travellers astronauts, Russians are cosmonauts and the South Africans (and Africans) afronauts. The Chinese word for space is *taikong*, and that is why the first Chinese space traveller, Yang Liwei, soon became known as a 'taikonaut'.

―――――― SOUTH AFRICA'S LARGEST TELESCOPE ――――――

- Sutherland in the Karoo is regarded as one of the coldest places in South Africa. It is also the home of the Southern African Large Telescope (SALT), which will be built over the next few years by South Africa and its German, Polish, American and New Zealand partners.

- The SALT project will cost about $30 million.

- It will be the largest single telescope in the southern hemisphere, with a hexagonal mirror array 11 m across.

- SALT is very similar to the Hobby-Eberly Telescope (HET) in Texas, but SALT will have a redesigned optical system, using more of the mirror array.

- SALT will be able to record distant stars, galaxies and quasars a billion times too faint to be seen with the unaided eye – as faint as a candle flame at the distance of the moon.

- It will 'see' back to a time when the universe was 10% of its current age, when the first galaxies were forming – around 1,5 billion years after the Big Bang. It will be recording light that was emitted 13,5 billion years ago and has taken that length of time to reach Earth, travelling a distance of $1{,}277\ 235 \times 10^{23}$ km in that time.

- SALT will provide information about the early history of the universe soon after the Big Bang, and also the detail needed about closer events – like detecting planets orbiting stars in our own galaxy.

- About 60% of the components used for SALT were made in South Africa, including the aluminium dome, the mirror segment mounts, and the mirror coating plant, which coats the mirror segments with aluminium.

- Namibia has the High Energy Stereoscopic System (HESS) gamma ray observatory, which will be the largest of its kind in the world when its second phase is completed.

- Sutherland is in the Roggeveld mountains in the Northern Cape. It was the birthplace of the writing Louw brothers, NP van Wyk Louw and WEG Louw. Both of them won the prestigious Hertzog Prize for Literature.
- Visitors to the historical Louw House in Sutherland can still see possessions of the two writers/poets, along with other cultural artefacts, such as a clay oven [*bakoond*] and a watermill.
- WEG Louw was named after William Ewart Gladstone, a four-time prime minister of Great Britain (1868–74, 1880–85, 1886, 1892–94).

SOUTH AFRICA'S BID FOR THE SKA (Square Kilometre Array)

- South Africa has submitted a bid to host the Square Kilometre Array (SKA). It is a massive radio telescope that will enable astronomers to probe the early evolution of our galaxy, about 14 billion years after the Big Bang, and will be an international project that will cost about $1 billion.
- According to the South African SKA bid, there are three sites in the Northern Cape that can host the SKA. All three have radio interference-free zones of 150 km (the requirement is 100-km radio interference-free areas). These sites are in the Kalahari, north of Upington, in the Karoo, north of Carnarvon, and in Namaqualand, east of Springbok.
- The project will create a receiving surface of a million square metres, one hundred times larger than the biggest receiving surface now in existence.
- This huge surface will be composed of many small antennas, divided into a dense inner-core array, which becomes more diffuse with increasing radius. The peripheral antennas could be 1 000 km from the core, or 5 000 km, or even 10 000 km, making the SKA an intercontinental system. The signals received by these antennas will be combined to form one single, big picture.
- The SKA radio telescope will have an effective collecting area of more than 30 times the largest telescope ever built.

SOUTH AFRICA'S COAT OF ARMS

South Africa's coat of arms consists of a series of elements, which are organised in two symmetric oval shapes, placed on top of one another.

The lower oval shape, representing the foundation, contains the following elements:

- The motto, in a green semicircle, is *!ke e: /xarra //ke*, written in the Khoisan language of the /Xam people, which means 'Diverse People Unite'.
- Two symmetrically placed pairs of elephant tusks pointing upwards. Elephants represent wisdom, strength, moderation and eternity.
- Two symmetrical ears of wheat, an emblem of fertility, which symbolises the idea of germination, growth and development of potential.
- A centrally placed gold shield, symbolic of identity and spiritual defence.
- A spear and a knobkerrie, crossed in a single unit, as symbols of defence and authority. They are shown horizontally to signify peace.
- Two human figures from Khoisan rock art, facing one another in greeting and in unity. The figures are from images on the Linton Stone, a world famous example of South African rock art, which can be seen in the South African Museum in Cape Town.

The higher oval shape, representing ascendancy, contains the following elements:
- A protea, with its petals arranged in a triangular pattern, reminiscent of the crafts of Africa. It is an emblem of the beauty of South Africa and the flowering of the nation's potential in pursuing the African Renaissance.
- A secretary bird, with its wings uplifted. The protea forms its chest. The secretary bird is a symbol of divine majesty, and its uplifted wings show the ascendance of the South African nation, and symbolise protection. The bird's golden colour represents its association with the sun and the highest power.
- A rising sun above the horizon, between the wings of the secretary bird. The sun is the source of life and light, and represents the ultimate wholeness of humanity.

Three designers presented their concepts to the cabinet, who eventually chose the design proposed by Iaan Bekker for the new coat of arms.

—————— THE SOUTH AFRICAN DEFENCE FORCE ——————

- General Jan Smuts was appointed Minister of the Interior, Mining and Defence in 1910, and he was largely responsible for drafting the Defence Act, which would be used to create a national defence force.
- This Defence Act was promulgated on 14 June 1912, and made provision for a Union Defence Force, which consisted of an Active Citizen Force, Rifle Associations, and a Permanent Force. Provision was also made for an Aviation Corps, a Coastal Defence Corps and a Cadet Corps for schools.
- The South African Air Force was formed in 1920, and the South African Naval Service in 1922.
- When South Africa took part in the First World War, a total of 275 000 South Africans (soldiers and auxiliary troops) fought in the various campaigns, and 12 452 were killed. South Africans won 2 403 decorations, which included 13 Victoria Crosses.
- A total of 400 000 South Africans took part in the Second World War, and 12 080 were killed. Members of the South African Defence Force received 7 114 decorations.
- The South African National Defence Force (SANDF) was formed on 26 April 1994, with members from a variety of different organisations – the South African Defence Force, MK, Apla, and the defence forces of the TBVC states.

—————— RANK STRUCTURE IN THE SOUTH AFRICAN ——————
NATIONAL DEFENCE FORCE (SANDF)

GENERAL OFFICERS OR FLAG OFFICERS

Rank	Abbre-viation	Description	Form of address	Navy equivalent
General	Gen	Highest commissioned rank in the Army, Air Force and Military Health Service, above Lieutenant General	General	Admiral
Lieutenant General	Lt Gen	Commissioned rank in the Army, Air Force and Military Health Service, below General and above Major General	General	Vice Admiral
Major General	Maj Gen	Commissioned rank in the Army, Air Force and Military Health Service, below Lieutenant General and above Brigadier General	General	Rear Admiral
Brigadier General	Brig Gen	Commissioned rank in the Army, Air Force and Military Health Service, below Major General and above Colonel	General	Rear Admiral (Junior Grade)

SENIOR OFFICERS

Rank	Abbreviation	Description	Form of address	Navy equivalent
Colonel	Col	Commissioned rank in the Army, Air Force and Military Health Service, below Brigadier General and above Lieutenant Colonel	Colonel	Captain
Lieutenant Colonel	Lt Col	Commissioned rank in the Army, Air Force and Military Health Service, below Colonel and above Major	Colonel	Commander
Major	Maj	Commissioned rank in the Army, Air Force and Military Health Service, below Lieutenant Colonel and above Captain	Major	Lieutenant Commander

JUNIOR OFFICERS

Rank	Abbreviation	Description	Form of address	Navy equivalent
Captain	Capt	Commissioned rank in the Army, Air Force and Military Health Service, below Major and above Lieutenant	Captain	Lieutenant
Lieutenant	Lt	Commissioned rank in the Army, Air Force and Military Health Service, below Captain and above Second Lieutenant	Lieutenant	Sub Lieutenant
Second Lieutenant	2 Lt	Lowest commissioned rank in the Army, Air Force and Military Health Service, below Lieutenant	Lieutenant	Ensign
Candidate Officer	CO	Member of the Army, Air Force and Military Health Service under training for officership		

WARRANT OFFICERS

Rank	Abbreviation	Description	Form of address	Navy equivalent
Warrant Officer	WO	An officer in the Army, Air Force, Navy or Military Health Service holding his/her rank by virtue of a Warrant	Sergeant Major	
Sergeant Major	Sgt Maj	Colloquial term for a Warrant Officer		

NON-COMMISSIONED OFFICERS

Rank	Abbreviation	Description	Form of address	Navy equivalent
Staff Sergeant	S Sgt	Non-commissioned rank in the Army and Military Health Service, below Warrant Officer and above Sergeant	Staff	Chief Petty Officer
Sergeant	Sgt	Non-commissioned rank in the Army, Air Force and Military Health Service, below Staff Sergeant and Flight Sergeant and above Corporal	Sergeant	Officer
Corporal	Cpl	Non-commissioned rank in the Army, Air Force and Military Health Service, below Sergeant and above Lance Corporal	Corporal	Leading Seaman

Rank	Abbreviation	Description	Form of address	Navy equivalent
Lance Corporal	L Cpl	Lowest non-commissioned rank in the Army, Air Force and Military Health Service, below Corporal	Corporal	Able Seaman
OTHER				
Flight Sergeant	F Sgt	Non-commissioned rank in the Air Force, below Warrant Officer and above Sergeant	Flight	Chief Petty Officer
Bombardier	Bdr	Non-commissioned rank in the Artillery Corps, equivalent to a Corporal in the Army	Bombardier	Leading Seaman
Lance Bombardier	L Bdr	Lowest non-commissioned rank in the Artillery, corresponding to Lance Corporal in the Infantry Corps	Bombardier	Able Seaman
SOLDIERS				
Private	Pte	The lowest rank in the Army and Military Health Service	Private	Seaman
Airman	Amn	The lowest rank in the Air Force (equivalent rank in the Army is Private)	Airman	Seaman
Gunner	Gnr	A soldier in the Artillery Corps	Gunner	
Pioneer	Pnr	A member in the Infantry doing duty tasks	Pioneer	
Rifleman	Rfn	A soldier in the Infantry Corps	Rifleman	
Sapper	Spr	A soldier in the Engineer Corps	Sapper	
Scout	Sct	A soldier in the Intelligence Corps	Scout	
Signalman	Smn	A soldier in the Signal Corps	Signalman	
Trooper	Tpr	A soldier in the Armour Corps	Trooper	

SA NAVY
GENERAL OFFICERS OR FLAG OFFICERS

Rank	Abbreviation	Description	Form of address
Admiral	Adm	Highest commissioned rank in the Navy, above Vice Admiral	Admiral
Vice Admiral	V Adm	Commissioned rank in the Navy, below Admiral and above Rear Admiral	Admiral
Rear Admiral	R Adm	Commissioned rank in the Navy, below Vice Admiral and above Rear Admiral (Junior Grade)	Admiral
Rear Admiral (Junior Grade)	R Adm (JG)	Commissioned rank in the Navy, below Rear Admiral and above Captain	Admiral

SENIOR OFFICERS

Rank	Abbreviation	Description	Form of address
Captain (SAN)	Capt (SAN)	Commissioned rank in the Navy, below Rear Admiral (Junior Grade) and above Commander	Captain
Commander	Cdr	Commissioned rank in the Navy, below Captain and above Lieutenant Commander	Commander
Lieutenant Commander	Lt Cdr	Commissioned rank in the Navy, below Commander and above Lieutenant	Commander

JUNIOR OFFICERS

Rank	Abbreviation	Description	Form of address
Lieutenant(SAN)	Lt(SAN)	Commissioned rank in the Navy, below Lieutenant Commander and above Sub Lieutenant	Lieutenant
Sub Lieutenant	S Lt	Commissioned rank in the Navy, below Lieutenant and above Ensign	Lieutenant
Ensign	Esn	Lowest commissioned rank in the Navy, below Sub Lieutenant	Ensign
Midshipman	Mid	A member of the Navy under training for officership	Midshipman

WARRANT OFFICER

Rank	Abbreviation	Description	Form of address
Warrant Officer	WO	An Officer in the Army, Air Force, Navy or Military Health Service holding his/her rank by virtue of a Warrant	Warrant

NON-COMMISSIONED OFFICERS

Rank	Abbreviation	Description	Form of address
Chief Petty Officer	CPO	Non-commissioned rank in the Navy, below Warrant Officer and above Petty Officer	Chief
Petty Officer	PO	Non-commissioned rank in the Navy, below Chief Petty Officer and above Leading Seaman	PO
Leading Seaman	LS	Non-commissioned rank in the Navy, below Petty Officer and above Able Seaman	Killick
Able Seaman	AB	Lowest non-commissioned rank in the Navy, below Leading Seaman	AB

SOLDIERS

Rank	Abbreviation	Description	Form of address
Seaman	Sea	The lowest rank in the Navy	Seaman

THE SOUTH AFRICAN
POLICE SERVICE (SAPS)

Rank structure

Rank	Form of address
National Commissioner	Commissioner
Deputy National Commissioner	Commissioner
Provincial Commissioner	Commissioner
Divisional Commissioner	Commissioner
Assistant Commissioner	Commissioner
Director	Director
Senior Superintendent	Superintendent
Superintendent	Superintendent
Captain	Captain
Inspector	Inspector
Sergeant	Sergeant
Constable	Constable

Did you know?

The total number of police officers in February 2004 was 106 364. The estimated population of the country, according to Statistics South Africa's mid-year estimate for 2002, was 45 454 211.

Provincial ratio of police officials to population

Province	Ratio
Eastern Cape	1 : 535
Free State	1 : 352
Gauteng	1 : 350
KwaZulu-Natal	1 : 551
Limpopo	1 : 748
Mpumalanga	1 : 564
Northern Cape	1 : 267
North West	1 : 486
Western Cape	1 : 413
National	1 : 427

Did you know?
* At the end of the 19th century, a number of independent urban and rural police agencies existed in South Africa, including colonial police forces such as the Cape Mounted Riflemen, the Cape Mounted Police, the Transvaal Police, the Natal Police and the Orange River Colony Police.
* After 1911 the Union police force was organised along the lines of the system used in the Cape Province. There were two different forces, the South African Police and the Mounted Riflemen.

- Proclamation 18 of 1913 named 1 April as the date for the founding of the South African Police. Colonel TG Truter was the first Commissioner of Police. A total of 5 882 policemen were employed in this force. In 1926, this total had nearly doubled to 10 195.

- The transport situation looked somewhat different at the beginning of the 20th century than today, because the police relied largely on animal transport. In 1915 the SA Police had 53 motor vehicles, 117 motorcycles, 3 679 horses, 527 mules, 96 donkeys, 37 oxen and 84 camels.

- The first police dogs were 'employed' in 1909 in Natal, and the police in Transvaal began using dogs in 1911. By 1920 the police had 65 dogs.

- After the first democratic election in 1994, the 11 different police forces in South Africa became one police force, the South African Police Services. General George Fivaz became the first national commissioner of police, and he was succeeded in 2001 by commissioner Jackie Selebi.

SOUTH AFRICAN SUBMARINES

- South Africa is the only African country to operate and maintain submarines.
- South Africa's first three submarines were named:
  - SAS *Johanna van der Merwe* (After a young Voortrekker girl who survived an attack on her group)
  - SAS *Emily Hobhouse* (After the English social worker in South Africa during the Anglo-Boer War), and
  - SAS *Maria van Riebeeck* (After the wife of Jan van Riebeeck, the first Dutch commander at the Cape)
- The three submarines were later renamed to:
  - SAS *Assegaai*
  - SAS *Umkhonto* (isiXhosa for 'assegai'), and
  - SAS *Spear.*
- The first of three new Type 209-class submarines, the S 101, was launched in Kiel, Germany, in 2004. The submarines are described as 'modern, conventionally-powered and highly capable' vessels. The combat system is of German design, but the components will be largely manufactured in South Africa. The first submarine will be delivered in 2005, the second in 2006 and the third in 2007.

SOUTH AFRICA'S NATIONAL ORDERS

South Africa's national orders are the highest awards that the country, through the president, can bestow on its citizens and foreign nationals.

∼ THE ORDER OF MAPUNGUBWE ∼

The Order of Mapungubwe is awarded to South African citizens for excellence and exceptional achievement.

Classes	Order
Class 1	The Platinum Order of Mapungubwe
Class 2	The Gold Order of Mapungubwe
Class 3	The Bronze Order of Mapungubwe

Did you know?

The Kingdom of Mapungubwe existed a thousand years ago in the northern part of South Africa, with a sophisticated state system, developed agriculture, and a mining and metallurgy industry. It traded with countries as far as China, and represented excellence of human thought and ingenuity.

∼ THE ORDER OF THE BAOBAB ∼

The Order of the Baobab is awarded to South African citizens for distinguished service, well above and beyond the ordinary call of duty.

Classes	Order	
Class 1	Supreme Counsellor of the Order of the Baobab	Gold
Class 2	Grand Counsellor of the Order of the Baobab	Silver
Class 3	Counsellor of the Order of the Baobab	Bronze

Did you know?

This order was inspired by the legendary baobab tree (*Adonsonia digitata*), which grows in tropical Africa, and is honoured for its vitality, and its magical and symbolic value to indigenous people. It provides bark for cloth and rope, fruits for food and fuel, and many other useful products, and is used for important meetings and protection in traditional African societies.

∼ THE ORDER OF THE COMPANIONS OF OR TAMBO

The Order of the Companions of OR Tambo is awarded to foreign nationals (heads of state and government) and other dignitaries, for friendship shown to South Africa. It is an order of peace, cooperation and active expression of solidarity and support.

Classes	Order
Class 1	Supreme Companion of OR Tambo
Class 2	Grand Companion of OR Tambo
Class 3	Companion of OR Tambo

Did you know?
Oliver Reginald Tambo (1917–1993), born in Bizana, Transkei, played a major role in the growth and development of the international movement of solidarity against racism and apartheid, establishing the first missions of the liberation movement in Egypt, Morocco, Ghana and London. He led the African National Congress while he was in exile from 1960 to 1990.

∼ ORDER OF LUTHULI ∼

The Order of Luthuli is awarded to South Africans who have made a meaningful contribution to the struggle for democracy, human rights, nation-building, justice and peace, and conflict resolution.

Category	Order
Category 1	Gold
Category 2	Silver
Category 3	Bronze

Did you know?
Chief Albert John Mavumbi Luthuli (1898–1967) was a legendary liberation struggle leader and the first African to receive the Nobel Peace Prize (1960).

∼ THE ORDER OF IKHAMANGA ∼

The Order of Ikhamanga is awarded to South African citizens who excel in the fields of arts, culture, literature, music, journalism and sport.

Category	Order
Category 1	Gold
Category 2	Silver
Category 3	Bronze

Did you know?
The ikhamanga (*Strelitzia*) is a plant which is also known as the crane flower or bird of paradise flower.

∼ THE MENDI DECORATION FOR BRAVERY ∼

The Mendi Decoration for Bravery is awarded to South African citizens who have performed an extraordinary act of bravery, which placed their lives in great danger, or who lost their own lives, including trying to save the life of another person, or

by saving property, in or outside the Republic of South Africa. It is awarded in three
categories:

Category	Order
Category 1	Gold
Category 2	Silver
Category 3	Bronze

Did you know?

- The SS *Mendi*, a 4 230-ton troopship, sank after being struck by the SS *Darro*
  near the Isle of Wight in the English Channel on 21 February 1917, during the
  First World War. The South African soldiers who drowned in the disaster were
  on their way to France to assist the British.
- The name SS *Mendi* was used again in 2004, this time for one of the SA Navy's
  new patrol corvettes.

——— SOUTH AFRICA'S LIGHTHOUSES ———

Record	Lighthouse
Strongest beam	Cape Point lighthouse, Cape Peninsula – 10 000 000 CD
Most isolated manned lighthouse	Dassen Island lighthouse – 11 km offshore
First automated lighthouse	Green Point lighthouse, KwaZulu-Natal – 1961
Only diaphone-type fog signal still operating	Cape Columbine lighthouse, West Coast
Tallest lighthouse tower	Slangkop lighthouse, Cape Peninsula
Northernmost lighthouse	Jesser Point, KwaZulu-Natal
Only lighthouse on a rock	Roman Rock, False Bay, Western Cape
Only female lighthouse keeper	Mrs Coward, St Lucia lighthouse, KwaZulu-Natal (1940s)
Most distinctive colour	Cape Vidal lighthouse, KwaZulu-Natal (yellow)

Portnet manages 46 lighthouses. Keepers operate 18, and 28 are automatic.

——— WORLD FAMOUS MUSICIANS AND PRODUCERS BORN IN SOUTH AFRICA ———

Trevor Rabin   Trevor Rabin was born in Johannesburg, and became a member of the group
Rabbitt, and later of Yes. He composed music for a number of international
movies: *The Great Raid* (2004), *Torque* (2004), *Bad Boys II* (2003), *Kangaroo Jack*
(2003), *Bad Company* (2002), *The Banger Sisters* (2002), *American Outlaws*
(2001), *The One* (2001), *Rock Star* (2001), *Texas Rangers* (2001), *Gone in 60
Seconds* (2000), *Remember the Titans* (2000), *The Sixth Day* (2000), *Whispers:
An Elephant's Tale* (2000), *Deep Blue Sea* (1999), *Armageddon* (1998), *Enemy of
the State* (1998), *Homegrown* (1998), *Jack Frost* (1998), *Con Air* (1997), *Soldiers of
Fortune Inc.* (1997), *The Glimmer Man* (1996) and *Twister* (1995).

Dave Matthews Singer/guitarist Dave Matthews was born in Johannesburg, but moved to the USA, where he put together the Dave Matthews Band (DMB). Their self-released debut, *Remember Two Things*, sold at a rate of more than 10 000 copies a month. Their major label debut (RCA) was *Under the Table and Dreaming*, produced by Steve Lillywhite (U2, Talking Heads, Rolling Stones). They also released *Crash* (1996), *Before These Crowded Streets* (1998), two double-CD live sets *Listener Supported* and *Live at Luther College* (1999), and *Everyday* (2001). Dave Matthews won a Grammy for Best Male Rock Vocal Performance for 'Gravedigger' from *Some Devil* at the 46th Annual Grammy Awards. The Dave Matthews Band was also awarded the special Chairman's Award at the NAACP Image Awards.

Richard Jon Smith Richard Jon Smith, singer, songwriter and record producer for various artists, was born in Cape Town, and helped to compose the music for *The Jewel of the Nile*, the sequel to *Romancing the Stone*, starring Michael Douglas and Kathleen Turner. He also composed nearly all his own hits, like 'Michael Row the Boat Ashore', 'Candlelight', 'Love', 'I'm Coming Home', 'Sweet Mama' and 'That's Why I Love You'.

Manfred Mann Manfred Mann was born as Manfred Lubowitz in Johannesburg, and formed the Mann/Hugg Blues Brothers in 1962. The name was changed to Manfred Mann, and the band played jazz and R&B-based rock, and later pop/rock and progressive rock. The name was later changed to Manfred Mann's Earth Band. Some of the group's hits are 'Pretty Flamingo', 'Sha La La', 'Do Wah Diddy Diddy', 'Mighty Quinn', 'Come Tomorrow', 'I'm Your Kingpin', 'Tired of Trying, Bored With Lying, Scared of Dying' and 'Oh No, Not My Baby'.

Duncan Faure Duncan Faure, singer and songwriter, as well as guitarist and keyboard player, was born in Pretoria. His first band was Orange Cash Boat, and he was an impor- tant member of the 1970s pop band Rabbitt (with Trevor Rabin as a member). He also made a huge contribution to the Bay City Rollers, the Scottish super band. In 1987 he contributed to Madonna's *Who's That Girl* soundtrack on the single '24 Hours'. George Benson performed 'Let It Be Right', a song Faure wrote, at the 1993 Miss World pageant. Some of his other hits were 'Ball and Chain', 'Brother', '24 Hours', 'Shining Star', 'I'm Gonna Make It', 'Better Than Ever', 'Lovelight', 'Everyday', 'You Gave Me Love' and 'Cry Out Love'.

Bill Drummond Bill Drummond was born in South Africa, but he grew up in Galloway and Corby in Scotland. He used different aliases, such as The Justified Ancients of Mumu and The Timelords. In 1977 he performed with the group Big in Japan, and later created a music business enterprise called The Zoo, acting as producer and label manager, and released the debuts of Echo and The Bunnymen and The Teardrop Explodes. He also started Zoo Records, and performed with The Woodentops and Zodiac Mindwarp. His solo project is titled *Bill Drummond – The Man*, and he now uses another alias – KLF.

Miriam Stockley Miriam Stockley was born in Johannesburg, and has worked with artists such as Tina Turner, Elton John, George Michael, Freddie Mercury, Chaka Khan, David Bowie and Seal. The Adiemus project, featuring Miriam's vocals, was recorded in 1995 with the London Philharmonic Orchestra, and released as *Songs of Sanctuary*, and together with the follow-ups, *Cantata Mundi* and *Dances of Time*, has sold more than 2 million copies worldwide. She also appeared live in the Wham! Final Concert and the Freddie Mercury Tribute Concert, and provided

	backing vocals for Elton John, Annie Lennox, David Bowie and Seal. Her debut solo, *Miriam*, was released in 1999.
Jonathan Butler	Jonathan Butler, guitarist and vocalist, was born in Cape Town, and was still a teenager when producer Clive Calder signed him to Jive Records in 1977, and produced *Introducing Jonathan Butler*, his debut album. He has made 12 more albums since then, which include *If You're Ready (Come Go With Me)*, *Say We'll Be Together, Sarah, Sarah, Love Songs, Candlelight and You, What Would You Do for Love?, Baby Please Don't Take It (I Need Your Love), I Found Myself in You, You Don't Belong to Me* and *The Way You Look Tonight*.
Bob Calvert	Robert Calvert was born in Pretoria. He went to London with his family and worked as a building surveyor before he linked up with the space-rock band Hawkwind. In 1972 he wrote their hit 'Silver Machine', and toured with the band before releasing his concept album *Captain Lockheed and the Starfighters* in 1974. In 1975 he wrote *The Stars That Play with Laughing Sam's Dice*, a drama based on the life of Jimi Hendrix. He rejoined Hawkwind for the LP *Quark, Strangeness and Charm*, and later formed the Hawklords, which recorded *25 Years On*. Calvert also recorded *Hype* (1982), *Freq* (1984) and *Test-Tube Conceived* (1986). He died in 1988.
Clive Calder	Clive Calder, bassist, band leader and businessman, was born in Johannesburg, but became a British citizen in 1975, and founded the independent record label Zomba, which signed up international stars such as Britney Spears, Backstreet Boys and 'N Sync, and South Africans such as Richard Jon Smith, Lionel Peterson and Jonathan Butler. Calder sold Zomba in 2002 to the German media giant BMG. In 2004, Calder dethroned Sir Paul McCartney as the richest person in the British music industry, with a net worth of £1,235 billion.

ARTISTS WHO HAVE CHANGED THEIR NAMES

It seems as if no artist is comfortable with his or her name any more, and when his or her first single spins in the CD drive (or even before that), a new, funky name will grace the jewel case – a name that will not be recognised by family and friends back home. The most extreme case of name changing must surely be that of He-who-was-born-as-Prince-Rogers-Nelson. That was Prince's real birth name in 1958, before all the fun and games started ...

In 1993, PRN changed his name to an unwritable symbol, and was popularly known as Symbol (for verily, the symbol was unpronounceable as well). He followed it with The Artist Formerly Known As Prince, abbreviated to TAFKAP, with The Artist as alternative. When nobody took any notice, he changed it back to Prince – but along the way he did threaten to change it to Britney Spears ... Maybe The Mind Boggles would be a better choice.

Interestingly, The Abovementioned Artist could play the keyboard, guitar, drums, saxophone and at least 10 other instruments by the time he finished high school.

South African artists have also clambered onto the name-changing bandwagon.

Artist	Real name
Abdullah Ibrahim (previously Dollar Brand)	Adolphus Johannes Brand
Alexis	Nicole Williams
Bernoldus Niemand	James Phillips
Billy Forrest	William Broadman
Bles Bridges	Lawrence John Gabriel Bridges
Bones Brettell	Ronald Brettell
Brendan Jury	Brendan Smit
Clive Bruce	Clive Bruce Bergman
Crocodile Harris	Robin Graham
David Marks	Spiros D Markantonatos
Die Baron	Daniel Lukas Heyneke
Gene Rockwell	Gert Francois Smit
Geoff St John	Geoffrey Jacobs
Glenys Lynne	Glenys Lynne Mynott
Jean-Michel Byron	Byron du Plessis
Joanna Field	Joan Elizabeth Lubbe
Johannes Kerkorrel	Ralph John Rabie
John Ireland	John Griffith
Karen Zoid	Karen Greeff
Koos Kombuis (André Letoit)	André Le Roux Du Toit
Kupido	Johannes Mattheus Wessels
Lance James	Lance James Liebenberg
Manfred Mann	Michael Lubowitz
Margino	Kim Kallie
Maritza	Brenda Ann du Preez
Marloe Scott-Wilson	Mandi Heyns
Mickie Most	Michael Hayes
Min Shaw	Wilhelmina Jacoba Viviers
Nataniël	Nataniël le Roux
Nianell	Sonia Nel
Nielen Mirror	Nielen Marais
Peter Vee	Peter Paoliello
PJ Powers	Penelope Jane Dunlop
Quentin E Klopjaeger	William Broadman
Quinsey	Alan Elderkin
Randy Rambo	Philippus Theunis Engelbrecht
Ronnie Robot	Ronald Friedman
Sally Vaughan	Susarah Viljoen
Sean Fury	Sean Fourie
Sharon Tandy	Sharon Finkelstein
Simon 'Agent' Orange	Simon Dunbar-Whittaker
Tolla van der Merwe	Tertius Willem Jacobus van der Merwe
Tully McCully	Terence McCullagh
Valiant Swart	Pierre Nolte
Virginia Lee	Virginia de Jager
Wanda Arletti	Wanda Arletowicz
Warrick Sony	Warrick Swinney
Willam E	William Broadman
Worsie Visser	Hermias Cornelius Visser
Yoti die Griekse Boertjie	Panayoti Loizos

---------- CHARLIZE THERON ----------

Charlize Theron is from Benoni, and is named after her father Charles. She began studying ballet at the age of six, and danced professionally in Johannesburg before becoming a fashion model at the tender age of 14. She is an outspoken animal lover, and her two cocker spaniels are named Denver and Delilah. She became the first South African to win a best actress Academy Award – in 2004, for *Monster*, a film that provided her with a cupboard full of other awards as well.

Year	Organisation	Award	Category/Recipient(s)
2004	Academy of Motion Picture Arts and Sciences	Oscar	Best Actress for: *Monster* (2003)
2004	Berlin International Film Festival	Silver Berlin Bear	Best Actress for: *Monster* (2003) *
2004	Broadcast Film Critics Association	BFCA Award	Best Actress for: *Monster* (2003)
2004	Chicago Film Critics Association	CFCA Award	Best Actress for: *Monster* (2003)
2004	Dallas–Forth Worth Film Critics Association	DFWFCA Award	Best Actress for: *Monster* (2003)
2004	Hollywood Foreign Press Association	Golden Globe	Best Performance by an Actress in a Motion Picture, Drama for: *Monster* (2003)
2004	International Press Academy	Golden Satellite Award	Best Performance by an Actress in a Motion Picture, Drama for: *Monster* (2003)
2004	Independent Spirit Awards	Independent Spirit Award	Best Female Lead for: *Monster* (2003)
2004	Las Vegas Film Critics Society	Sierra Award	Best Actress for: *Monster* (2003)
2003	National Board of Review, USA	NBR Award	Best Breakthrough Performance by an Actress for: *Monster* (2003)
2004	National Society of Film Critics Awards, USA	NSFC Award	Best Actress for: *Monster* (2003)
2003	San Francisco Film Critics Circle	SFFCC Award	Best Actress for: *Monster* (2003)
2004	Screen Actors Guild	SAG Award	Outstanding Performance by a Female Actor in a Leading Role for: *Monster* (2003)
2004	Vancouver Film Critics Circle	VFCC Award	Best Actress for: *Monster* (2003)

* Tied with Catalina Sandino Moreno for *María, llena Eres de Gracia* (2004).

---------- SOUTH AFRICANS AND THE OSCARS ----------

Person	Movie	Year	Category	Won/Nominated	Award
Charlize Theron	*Monster*	2004	Best Actress	Won	Academy Award
Ronald Harwood	*The Pianist*	2003	Best Writing (Screenplay based on material previously produced or published)	Won	Academy Award

Person	Movie	Year	Category	Won/Nominated	Award
Justine Shapiro	*Promises*	2002	Best documentary, Features	Nominated	Academy Award
Stephen Goldblatt	*Batman Forever*	1996	Best Cinematography	Nominated	Academy Award
Stephen Goldblatt	*The Prince of Tides*	1992	Best Cinematography	Nominated	Academy Award
Ronald Harwood	*The Dresser*	1984	Best Writing (Screenplay Based on Material from Another Medium)	Nominated	Academy Award
Cecil Kellaway	*Guess Who's Coming to Dinner*	1968	Best Actor in a Supporting Role	Nominated	Academy Award
Cecil Kellaway	*The Luck of the Irish*	1949	Best Actor in a Supporting Role	Nominated	Academy Award
Ian Dalrymple	*Pygmalion*	1939	Best Writing, Screenplay	Nominated	Academy Award
Ian Dalrymple	*The Citadel*	1939	Best Writing, Screenplay	Nominated	Academy Award
Basil Rathbone	*If I Were King*	1939	Best Actor in a Supporting Role	Nominated	Academy Award
Basil Rathbone	*Romeo and Juliet*	1937	Best Actor in a Supporting Role	Nominated	Academy Award

Most Oscars won by a film

- Three films have won 11 Oscars. The most recent is Peter Jackson's *The Lord of the Rings: The Return of the King* (USA/NZ, 2003), the third part of the *Lord of the Rings* trilogy. The movie – the fastest to gross $1 billion, taking just nine weeks and four days – won every award it was nominated for, a feat not achieved since Bernardo Bertolucci's *The Last Emperor* (1987).
- *Titanic* (USA, 1997) won 11 of the 14 Oscars it was nominated for in 1998.
- The first film to achieve the record of 11 Oscars was *Ben-Hur* (USA, 1959), which was nominated for 12 Oscars in 1959.

Oscar trivia

The Oscar statuette ...

... is 34 cm high

... weighs nearly 4 kg

... stands on a roll of film

... has a sword in its hand

... consists of iron, copper, nickel, silver and 24-carat gold, and is made in a factory in Chicago.

SOUTH AFRICA'S OLYMPIC
GOLD MEDAL WINNERS

Name	Year	Venue	Sport	Event
Reginald Walker	1908	London	Athletics	100 m Men
Kennedy Kane McArthur	1912	Stockholm	Athletics	Marathon Men
Rudolph Lewis	1912	Stockholm	Cycling Road	Individual time trial Men
Harry Austin Kitson	1912	Stockholm	Tennis	Doubles Men
Charles Lyndhurst Winslow	1912	Stockholm	Tennis	Doubles Men
Charles Lyndhurst Winslow	1912	Stockholm	Tennis	Singles Men
Bevil Gordon D'Urban Rudd	1920	Antwerp	Athletics	400 m Men
Clarence Leonard Walker	1920	Antwerp	Boxing	50,8–53,52 kg (bantamweight) Men
Louis Raymond	1920	Antwerp	Tennis	Singles Men
William H Smith	1924	Paris	Boxing	50,8–53,52 kg (bantamweight) Men
Sidney Atkinson	1928	Amsterdam	Athletics	110 m hurdles Men
Lawrence Stevens	1932	Los Angeles	Boxing	57,15–61,24 kg (lightweight) Men
David Daniel Carstens	1932	Los Angeles	Boxing	72,57–79,38 kg (light-heavyweight) Men
Gerald Dreyer	1948	London	Boxing	58–62 kg (lightweight) Men
George Hunter	1948	London	Boxing	73–80 kg (light-heavyweight) Men
Esther Cornelia Brand	1952	Helsinki	Athletics	High jump Women
Joan Cynthia Harrison	1952	Helsinki	Swimming	100 m backstroke Women
Josia Thugwane	1996	Atlanta	Athletics	Marathon Men
Penelope Heyns	1996	Atlanta	Swimming	100 m breaststroke Women
Penelope Heyns	1996	Atlanta	Swimming	200 m breaststroke Women
SA Team	2004	Athens	Swimming	4 x 400 m freestyle relay Men

Roland Schoeman
Lyndon Ferns
Darian Townsend
Ryk Neethling

OLYMPIC HOST CITIES
AND MASCOTS

The Olympic Games take place every four years. What is now a multi-billion-dollar exercise was once, many millennia ago, a prestigious event attended only by males. The athletes took part in their birthday suits – a good reason for the total ban on women. The ancient Olympic Games began in 776 BC in Greece, and went on until the Roman Emperor Theodosius I abolished it in 393 AD. It resumed in 1896 in Athens, Greece, where it was again hosted in 2004.

Year	Host city	Host country	Mascot(s)
1896	Athens	Greece	
1900	Paris	France	
1904	St Louis	USA	
1908	London	United Kingdom	
1912	Stockholm	Sweden	
1916	First World War	–	
1920	Antwerp	Belgium	
1924	Paris	France	
1928	Amsterdam	Netherlands	
1932	Los Angeles	USA	
1936	Berlin	Germany	
1940	Second World War	–	
1944	Second World War	–	
1948	London	United Kingdom	
1952	Helsinki	Finland	
1956	Melbourne	Australia	
1960	Rome	Italy	
1964	Tokyo	Japan	
1968	Mexico City	Mexico	The peace dove (unofficial) Red jaguar (no name)
1972	Munich	West Germany	Waldi, the dachshund
1976	Montreal	Canada	Amik, the beaver
1980	Moscow	Soviet Union	Misha, the bear Vigri, a seal cub
1984	Los Angeles	USA	Sam, the eagle
1988	Seoul	South Korea	Hodori and Hosuni, a male and female tiger cub
1992	Barcelona	Spain	Cobi, a mountain sheepdog
1996	Atlanta	USA	Izzy, a Whatizit cartoon character
2000	Sydney	Australia	Syd, the duckbilled platypus Millie, the echidna Olly, the kookaburra
2004	Athens	Greece	Phevos and Athena (brother and sister)*
2008	Beijing	People's Republic of China	

* The names of two Olympian gods, Phevos (one of the names of Apollo, the Greek god), god of light and music, and Athena, the goddess of wisdom and patron of the city of Athens. Phevos and Athena represent the link between Greek history and the modern Olympic Games.

ATHLETICS WORLD RECORDS
HELD BY SOUTH AFRICANS

Men				
Athlete	Event	Time/Distance	Place	Date
Vincent Duncker	120 yards hurdles	15,0*	Pietermaritzburg	17 April 1909
George Weightman-Smith	110 m hurdles	14,8*	Amsterdam	31 July 1928
George Weightman-Smith	110 m hurdles	14,6	Amsterdam	31 July 1928
Danie Joubert	100 yards	9,4	Grahamstown	16 May 1931
Gert Potgieter	440 yards hurdles	50,7	Queenstown	20 April 1957
Gert Potgieter	440 yards hurdles	49,7	Cardiff	22 July 1958
Gert Potgieter	440 yards hurdles	49,3	Bloemfontein	16 April 1960
Paul Nash	100 m	10,0	Krugersdorp	2 April 1968
Marcello Fiasconaro[1]	800 m	1:43,7	Milan	27 June 1973
Danie Malan	1 000 m	2:16,0	Munich	24 June 1973
Sydney Maree[2]	1 500 m	3:31,24	Cologne	28 August 1973
John van Reenen	Discus	68,48 m	Stellenbosch	14 April 1975

* Equals record
1 Marcello Fiasconaro set this record while he was an Italian citizen.
2 Sydney Maree set his record after he had become an American citizen.

Women				
Athlete	Event	Time/Distance/ Height	Place	Date
Marjorie Clarke	High jump	1,60 m (5 ft 3 in)	London	23 June 1928
Marjorie Clarke	80 m hurdles	12,2	Pietermaritzburg	24 May 1930
Marjorie Clarke	80 m hurdles	12,0	Pietermaritzburg	2 April 1931
Marjorie Clarke	80 m hurdles	11,8	Pietermaritzburg	2 April 1931
Barbara Burke	100 yards	11,0	Pretoria	20 April 1935
Barbara Burke	220 yards	24,8	Pretoria	22 April 1935
Barbara Burke	80 m hurdles	11,6	Berlin	1 August 1937
Esther van Heerden (later Brand)	High jump	1,66 m (5ft 5 ⅜ in)	Stellenbosch	29 March 1941
SA Team Florence Wills Sally Black Edna Maskell Daphne Robb	4 x 110 yards	47,3	Kimberley	10 April 1950
SA Team Florence Wills Sally Black Edna Maskell Daphne Robb	4 x 110 yards	46,9	Pretoria	26 April 1950
Zola Budd	5 000 m	15:01,83	Stellenbosch	5 January 1984
Zola Budd[1]	2 000 m	5:33,15	England	13 July 1984
Zola Budd[1]	5 000 m	14:48,07	London	26 August 1985
Elana Meyer	15 km Road race	46:57	Cape Town	2 November 1991
Elana Meyer	Half marathon	1:06,44	Tokyo	15 January 1999

1 Zola Budd set her world records after becoming a British citizen.

---------------------- THE NATIONAL FLAG ----------------------

Development and specifications

• Fred Brownell, South Africa's state herald, designed South Africa's national flag, and it was first used on 27 April 1994.

• The central design of the flag is a convergent line, which begins as two white lines at the top and bottom left of the flag. It symbolises the coming together of diverse elements within South African society, which unite on the way forward. This theme of convergence and unity ties in with the motto 'Unity is Strength' on the previous South African coat of arms, and the current motto '*!ke e: /xarra //kè*', which means 'Diverse People Unite'.

• The colour specifications of the textile used for flags are as follows:

Green   Spectrum green (CKS 42)
Black   Blue black (CKS 401)
White   National flag white (CKS 701)
Gold   Gold yellow (CKS 724)
Red   Chilli red (CKS 750)
Blue   National flag blue (CKS 762)

The size of the national flag

• For official use, the proportion of the breadth to the length of the national flag should be the same as 2 to 3

• The national flags ...

   o   used at the Union Buildings and Tuynhuys are 360 cm × 540 cm

   o   used on ceremonial occasions have to be 270 cm × 180 cm, or larger (according to the size of the building)

   o   for ordinary use are 270 cm × 180 cm, or 180 cm × 120 cm (according to the size of the building)

   o   used during stormy weather are 90 cm × 60 cm.

Displaying the national flag

When the national flag is displayed together with ...

   o   any other flags, it must be hoisted first and lowered last

   o   national flags of other countries, all the flags should be of approximately equal size and flown at an equal height, and the South African flag must be on the right side of the building or platform (on the left side from the observer's point of view)

o   any other flags, which are not national flags, on separate flagstaffs, the national flag must be in the middle or on the left side from the observer's point of view or at the highest point of the group.

The national flag must be treated with respect. It must not …
o   touch the floor or the ground;
o   be used as a tablecloth or be draped in front of a platform;
o   be used to cover a statue, plaque, cornerstone, etc. at unveiling or similar ceremonies; or
o   be used to start or finish any competition, race or similar event.

BATTING AND BOWLING: THE OTHER WAY ROUND

There are quite a number of South African cricketers (international and provincial) who bat right-handed and bowl left-handed, or vice versa.

Bats left-handed, bowls right-handed		Bats right-handed, bowls left-handed	
International	**Provincial**	**International**	**Provincial**
Kepler Wessels	Carl Bradfield	Paul Adams	Lloyd Ferreira
Gary Kirsten	Arno Jacobs	Claude Henderson	Ross Veenstra
Graeme Pollock	Neil Johnson	Clive Eksteen	
Lance Klusener	Russel Symcox	Pieter Strydom	
Graeme Smith	Geoffrey Toyana	Morné van Wyk	
Albie Morkel	Vaughn van Jaarsveld		
JP Duminy	Kosie Venter		

CRICKETING BROTHERS

Brother 1	Brother 2	Brother 3
Philip Hands	Reggie Hands	
Tony Pithey	David Pithey	
Peter Pollock	Graeme Pollock	
William Richards	Alf Richards	
Eric Rowan	Atholl Rowan	
Stanley Snooke	Sibley Snooke	
AB Tancred	Louis Tancred	Vincent Tancred
George Tapscott	Lionel Tapscott	
Dan Taylor	Herby Taylor	
Herbert Wade	Walter Wade	
Peter Kirsten	Gary Kirsten	

---------- CRICKETING FATHERS AND SONS ----------

Father	Son
Frank Hearne	George Hearne
Johnny Lindsay	Dennis Lindsay
Dave Nourse	Dudley Nourse
Peter Pollock	Shaun Pollock
Len Tuckett	Lindsay Tuckett

---------- SPRINGBOK FATHERS AND SONS ----------

Father	Son
Alf Walker	Harry Walker
Mauritz van den Berg	Derek van den Berg
Felix du Plessis	Morné du Plessis
Louis Schmidt	Uli Schmidt
Moaner van Heerden	Wikus van Heerden
Schalk Burger	Schalk Burger (junior)

---------- SPRINGBOK BROTHERS ----------

Brother 1	Brother 2	Brother 3
Oupa Versfeld	Hasie Versfeld	
Sommie Morkel	Dougie Morkel	
Paul Roos	Gideon Roos	
Anton Stegmann	Jan Stegmann	
Arthur Marsberg	Archie Marsberg	
John Luyt	Dick Luyt	Freddie (Lammetjie) Luyt
Gerhard Morkel	Jacky Morkel	
Bennie Osler	Sharkey Osler	
JC van der Westhuizen	Ponie van der Westhuizen	
Boy Louw	Fanie Louw	
Jaap Bekker	Dolf Bekker	Martiens Bekker
Charlie Cockrell	Robert Cockrell	
Ian McCallum	Roy McCallum	
Polla Fourie	Carel Fourie	
Joggie Jansen	Eben Jansen	
Jackie Snyman	Dawie Snyman	
Darius Botha	Naas Botha	
Willie du Plessis	Michael du Plessis	Carel du Plessis
Helgard Muller	Pieter Muller	
Geo Cronjé	Jacques Cronjé	

PLAYING IN DIFFERENT POSITIONS

Dr Danie Craven (who was born Daniel Hartman Craven in Lindley) was a very versatile player. In his career of 16 tests he played in no fewer than four different positions. He started as **scrumhalf**, and played in that position in his first six tests. In his seventh test he was selected to play inside **centre** (against Australia), and the next week he was scrumhalf again. In his ninth test, on 26 June 1937, he played **flyhalf** against Australia, and in his next test he was **eighthman**, then flyhalf (and captain) against New Zealand, and in the following test (also against New Zealand) he returned to scrumhalf, a position he played in for the rest of his test career (three tests against the British Isles in 1938). Craven also played **fullback** for the Springboks in a tour match.

Did you know?

- Danie Craven served Springbok rugby on all levels. He was selected for the Springboks when he was only 20, and before he played for Western Province. He was also a national selector and coach, manager of the Springbok team and from 1956 president of the South African Rugby Board. When the South African Rugby Football Union (SARFU) replaced the South African Rugby Board, Craven and Ebrahim Patel were named co-chairpersons, a position he held until his death in 1993.

- Danie Craven was the first professor in Physical Education at the University of Stellenbosch, and he also received three doctorates – in Social Anthropology, Psychology and Physical Education.

- His loyal dog was called Bliksem [Lightning], and a statue to honour the two of them can still be seen at Coetzenburg in Stellenbosch.

INTERESTING RUGBY NICKNAMES

Bloues Volschenk	Boela du Plooy	Hakkies Husselman
Draadkar de Lange	Kapstok van Greuning	Bakkies Botha
Balie Swart	Domkrag Erasmus	Vleis Visagie
Boland Coetzee	Baksteen Nell	Vaatjie Nel
Bees Bouwer	Kleinjan Tromp	Slang Roux
Bok Markram	Boeta Wessels	Hasie Versfeldt
Skilpad Eloff	Wa Lamprecht	Mannetjies Roux
Barabas Venter	Takkies Reitz	Dagga Bosman
Kierie Barnard	Viervoet Liebenberg	China Bell
Japan le Roux	Kuifie van der Merwe	Kabous van der Westhuizen
Bulldog Fourie	Haas van Zyl	Sirkusleeu Kotzé
Spanjool Wessels	Faffa Knoetze	Gaffie du Toit

—— SPRINGBOKS: BEST-REPRESENTED SURNAME ——

The following surnames are best represented among the more than 600 players who have worn the Springbok jersey:

Surname	Players
Morkel	10
Du Plessis	9
Smith	7
Botha	6
De Villiers	6
Du Toit	6
Louw	6
Muller	6
Van der Merwe	6
Van Zyl	6

—— SOUTH AFRICANS PLAYING TEST RUGBY ——
FOR OTHER COUNTRIES

Name	Team	Years
Cuthbert Mullins	British Isles	1896
Jimmy McDonald	Scotland	1903–1905
Harold McCowat	Scotland	1905
Frederick John Hopley	England	1907–1908
Jas Davey	England	1908–1909
Rupert Williamson	England	1908–1909
Reggie Hands	England	1910
Stephen Steyn	Scotland	1911–1912
Walter Dickson	Scotland	1912–1913
Jan Krige	England	1920
Frank Mellish	England	1920–1921
Danie Erasmus	Australia	1923
Jack Gage	Ireland	1926–1927
Brian Black	England	1930–1933
Kenneth Marshall	Scotland	1934–1937
Tuppy Owen-Smith	England	1934–1937
Trilby Freakes	England	1938–1939
Mickey Davies	Wales	1939
Ossie Newton-Thompson	England	1947
Clive van Ryneveld	England	1949
Syd Newman	England	1947–1948
Murray Hofmeyr	England	1950
Harry Small	England	1950
Keith McMillan	Scotland	1953
Tug Wilson	England	1953–1954
Chick Henderson	Scotland	1953–1954
Nic Labuschagne	England	1953–1955
Kim Elgie	Scotland	1954–1955
Donald McDonald	Scotland	1977–1978

Name	Team	Years
Tito Lupini	Italy	1987–1989
Marcello Cuttita	Italy	1987–1999
Eric Melville	France	1990–1991
Massimo Cuttita	Italy	1990–2000
John Allan	Scotland	1990–1991
Christian Stewart	Canada	1991–1995
Graham Downes	USA	1992
Andries van Heerden	France	1992
Mike Catt	England	1994–
Matt Alexander	USA	1995–1998
Juan Grobler	USA	1996–2002
Matthew Proudfoot	Scotland	1998
André Blom	USA	1998–2000
Dion O'Cuinneagain	Ireland	1998–2000
Wim Visser	Italy	1999–2002
Pieter de Villiers	France	1999–
Tiaan Strauss	Australia	1999
Phillip Eloff	USA	2000–
Steve White-Cooper	England	2001
Giovani Antoni	Italy	2001
Roland Reid	Scotland	2001
Andy Marinos	Wales	2002–2003
Steven Hall	France	2002
Gert Peens	Italy	2002–2003
Dan Vickerman	Australia	2002–
Michael Horak	England	2002–
Geoff Appleford	England	2002–
Bloues Volschenk	Russia	2002–
Werner Pieterse	Russia	2002–
Tenk Hendricks	Russia	2002–
Conrad Breytenbach	Russia	2002–
Jurie Gouws	USA	2003–
Riaan van Zyl	USA	2003–
Hal Luscombe	Wales	2003–
Brian Liebenberg	France	2003–
Stuart Abbott	England	2003–
Gerhard Klerck	USA	2003–
Roland de Marigny	Italy	2004–
Fraser Waters	England	2004–
Matt Stevens	England	2004–
Clyde Rathbone	Australia	2004–
Shaun Payne*	Ireland	2004–

* Selected for touring teams, but not for tests

THE ALL BLACK HAKA

- Springbok teams have been facing the traditional haka since 1921, when they played their first test against New Zealand's All Blacks.
- 'Haka' is the generic name for all Maori dances. The haka used today is defined as that part of the Maori dance repertoire where the men are in the foreground,

with the women lending vocal support in the rear. Most of the current haka are *haka taparahi*, which means 'haka without weapons'.

- The word 'haka' consists of two parts: 'ha-ka'. 'Ha' means 'breath' and 'ka' means 'to ignite, to energise'.

- According to Maori mythology, the Sun God, Tama-nui-to-ra, had two wives, the summer maid, Hine-raumati, and the winter maid, Hine-takurua. The child of Tama-nui-to-ra and Hine-raumati, Tane-rore, is credited with the origin of the haka dance.

- The haka is still of significant social importance when the Maori welcome and entertain visitors, and a tribe's reputation is measured by their ability to perform the haka.

- Some elements essential to the art of haka are *pukana* (dilating of the eyes), *whetero* (protruding of the tongue) and *ngangahu* (similar to pukana). These expressions are used to lend meaning and force to the words.

- All Black rugby teams use the 'Ka mate, ka mate' haka. The words *ka mate* mean 'It's death'.

- This particular haka dates back to the early 19th century, when Chief Te Rauparaha of the Ngati Toa tribe, north of Waikato, was chased by enemies. He was allowed to hide in a *kumara* pit by Te Wharerangi, who was quite a hairy fellow, according to local legends. (*Kumara* are sweet potatoes, which were often harvested and stored in a pit to keep them dry.) Te Rauparaha was so relieved to be alive that he composed and performed a haka, which began with the words '*Ka mate! Ka mate! Ka ora! Ka ora!*'

- This is the haka always used by All Black rugby teams before the kick-off. Here is what they say, as well as a translation:

The words of the All Black haka	Translation
Ringa pakia	Slap the hands against the thighs
Uma tiraha	Puff out the chest
Turi whatia	Bend the knees
Hope whai ake	Let the hip follow
Waewae takahia kia kino*	Stamp the feet as hard as you can
Ka mate! Ka mate! Ka ora! Ka ora!	It's death! It's death! It's life! It's life!
Ka mate! Ka mate! Ka ora! Ka ora!	It's death! It's death! It's life! It's life!
Tenei te tangata puhuru huru	This is the hairy man
Nana nei i tiki mai	Who fetched the Sun
Whakawhiti te ra	And caused it to shine again
A upa ... ne! ka upa ... ne!	One upward step! Another upward step!
A upane kaupane whiti te ra!	An upward step, another ... the Sun shines!!
Hi !!!	Hi !!!

* The leader of the haka says the first five lines just prior to everyone performing it, to remind the performers how to behave when they do the haka.

Did you know?

• The first time the haka was used in an overseas representative match was in 1888–89, when it was performed by the New Zealand Native Team who toured the UK. This team was the first New Zealand team to wear a black jersey with a silver fern on the left breast.

• In 1905 the first official overseas tour ever by a representative New Zealand rugby team took place when 'The Originals' visited Britain. The name 'All Blacks' was coined on this tour, and the haka was performed for the first time by a team with that name.

• The three Pacific Island teams also have their own pre-match performances, similar to the All Black haka:

  o The Fijians call their war dance the *Cibi* (pronounced 'thimbi'), and it begins with the words, '*Ai tei vovo, tei vovo!*' ['Make ready, make ready!'].

  o The Tongans start their matches with the *Sipi Tau*, nicknamed the *Ikale Tahi*, or Sea Eagle. It starts with the words: '*Ei e! Ei e! Teu lea pea tala ki mamani katoa, Ko e 'ikale taki kuo halofia*', which means 'I shall speak to the whole world, The sea eagle is starved, Let the foreigner and sojourner beware.'

  o The Samoan team's challenge is called the *Siva Tau*. They composed it for the 1991 Rugby World Cup, to replace the 'gentler' *Ma'ulu'ulu Moa* on tour. It begins with the line, '*Le Manu Samoa e, ia manú le fai o le faiva*', meaning 'The Manu Samoa, may you succeed in your mission.'

——— SPRINGBOKS SENT OFF IN TESTS ———

	Player	Opponents	Referee	Venue	Date
1	James Small	Australia	EF Morrison (England)	Brisbane	14 August 1993
2	James Dalton	Canada	DTM McHugh (Ireland)	Port Elizabeth	3 June 1995
3	André Venter	New Zealand	WD Bevan (Wales)	Auckland	9 August 1997
4	Brendan Venter	Uruguay	PL Marshall (Australia)	Glasgow	15 October 1999
5	Marius Joubert	Australia	PD O'Brien (New Zealand)	Johannesburg	17 August 2002
6	Jannes Labuschagne	England	PD O'Brien (New Zealand)	Twickenham	23 November 2002

1 Small was sent off for backchatting the referee.

2 Dalton (and two Canadians) received their marching orders after a free-for-all broke out.

3 André Venter received his red card for allegedly stamping on the face of the All Black captain, Sean Fitzpatrick.

4 Brendan Venter was sent packing for allegedly kicking Uruguay's flank Martin Panizzi on the head in a ruck.

5 Marius Joubert was red-carded for a high tackle on Australia's Matt Rogers.

6 Jannes Labuschagne was sent off after a late tackle on England's Jonny Wilkinson.

MISS SOUTH AFRICA

- Winnie Comyns of Cape Town won a Miss SA title in 1926, in a national contest organised by the *SA Lady's Pictorial*. The queen of the Orange Free State was Blanca Borckenhagen; Ethel Jagger was queen of the Cape; Gyn Hathorn queen of Natal; and Blanca van der Hoven, queen of the Transvaal. The Cape Town city council banned beauty competitions in 1927 because 'they are undignified and not for the good of the city'.
- Avelyn 'Tootie' Macaskill of Bloemfontein was crowned as Miss SA in 1948, by nobody less than General Jan Smuts, at a ceremony at the Johannesburg City Hall.
- Catherine Higgins, a short-hand typist from Johannesburg, was chosen to represent South Africa at the first Miss Universe pageant in Long Beach, California, in 1952. She came 7th, and the other contestants named her 'Miss Friendly Spirit'.
- The official Miss South Africa competitions only began in 1956.

Year	Miss South Africa	Year	Miss South Africa
1956	Norma Vorster	1980	Sandra McCrystal
1957	Adéle Kruger	1981	Linda Phillips
1958	Penelope Ann (Penny) Coelen	1982	Sandra de Meyer
1959	Moya Meaker	1983	(No Pageant)
1960	Denise Muir	1984	Lorna Potgieter
1961	Yvonne Hulley	1985	Andrea Stelzer
1962	Yvonne Ficker	1986	Sandy McCormack
1963	Louise Crous	1987	Wilma van der Bijl
1964	Vedra Karamitas	1988	Janine Botbyl
1965	Carol Davis	1989	Michelle Bruce
1966	Joan Carter	1990	Suzette van der Merwe
1967	Disa Duivenstein	1991	Diana Tilden-Davis
1968	Mitzi Stander	1992	Amy Kleinhans
1969	Linda Collett	1993	Palesa Jacqueline Mofokeng
1970	Jillian Jessup	1994	Basetsane Julia Makgalemele
1971	Monica Fairall	1995	Bernalee Daniel
1972	Stephanie Reynecke	1996	Peggy-Sue Khumalo
1973	Shelly Latham	1997	Kerishnie Naicker
1974	Anneline Kriel	1998	Sonia Raciti
1975	Vera Johns	1999	Heather Joy Hamilton
1976	Lynne Massyn	2000	Jo-Ann Cindy Strauss
1977	Vanessa Wannenburg	2001	Vanessa Do Ceu Carreira
1978	Yolanda Kloppers	2002	Cindy Nell
1979	Karen Sickel	2003	Joan Ramagoshi

Did you know?

- Penny Coelen was crowned Miss World in 1958, and in 1974 Anneline Kriel became the second South African to win this title.
- Margaret Gardiner, another South African beauty, was crowned Miss Universe in 1978.

--- EVITA BEZUIDENHOUT ---

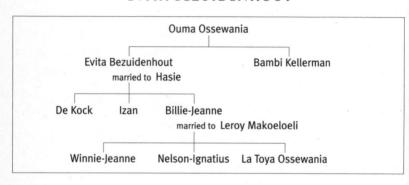

Name	Full names	Relationship to Evita	Biographic details
Evita Bezuidenhout	Evangelie Poggenpoel	–	Born: Bethlehem, 28 September 1935. Married to: JJ de V (Hasie). Became SA ambassadress to the Republic of Bapetikosweti (independent black homeland) in 1983. Assisted Pik Botha in the Total Diplomatic Onslaught on the world during the 1980s. Currently ambassador without portfolio, and chief liaison with regard to Afrikaans cultural affairs.
Bambi Kellerman	Sarie Poggenpoel (1938–)	Evita's younger sister	Born in Bethlehem, bred in Braamfontein. Married: Berchtesgaden (to a Nazi husband, now deceased; she keeps his ashes in an urn on her piano). Occupation: Brothel madam in the Paarl.
Ouma Ossewania	Ossewania Kakebenia Poggenpoel (1900–)	Evita's mother	Doesn't speak English.
Hasie	Johannes Jakobus de Villiers Bezuidenhout (1926–)	Evita's husband	Former MP for Laagerfontein; currently writing his (somewhat *deurmekaar*) autobiography.

Name	Full names	Relationship to Evita	Biographic details
De Kock	De Kock Bezuidenhout	Evita's son	Izan's twin brother. Very ... artistic. Member of the Gay Liberation Movement.
Izan	Izan Bezuidenhout	Evita's other son	De Kock's twin brother. Strong, mysterious, rides a massive, huge Kawasaki. Member of the AWB.
Billie-Jeanne	Billie-Jeanne Bezuidenhout (1963–)	Evita's only daughter	Dancer at the Glitter Pit Amphidome. Married to Leroy Makoeloeli, and has three children, Winnie-Jeanne, Nelson-Ignatius and La Toya Ossewania.

EVITA BEZUIDENHOUT

Evita and family's public appearances

Concentration Camp
Swartland Blondes
Bambi Sings the F.A.K. songs
The Poggenpoel Sisters
Bambi's Xmas Kê
Ouma Ossewania Praat Vuil
Skating on Thin Uys
Dekaffirnated
Farce about Uys
Adapt or Dye
Beyond the Rubicon
Total Onslaught
Tannie Evita Praat Kaktus
Tannie Evita's Cooksisters
Foreign Aids
The End is Naai

Books

A part hate, a part love
Evita's Funigalore
The Essential Evita Bezuidenhout
Elections and Erections

Did you know?

- Evita Bezuidenhout is the stage personality of Pieter-Dirk Uys, who is the brother of concert pianist Tessa Uys.
- Evita can be seen at 'Evita se Perron' over weekends. The name refers to Evita Perón (Argentina's first lady from 1946 to 1952); the word *perron* also means 'station platform' in Afrikaans.
- The small tin building is known as Die Wagkamer [The Waiting Room], and the art deco furniture is surround by a collection of Boere kitsch. You could also visit The Cafe Theatre and Berlin Bar, across the courtyard, and the kitchen specialises in boerekos, like bobotie, koeksisters, melktert, droëwors and biltong.
- The arts ands crafts building is known as Tannie Evita's A and C. Die Boekie-Hoekie [The Book Corner] sells South African books, and you can expect a Perron

- cat to come and sit on your lap there. There are 11 of them, and they have names like Moggie, Marilyn, Ginger, Boesman, Bambi, Elsie, Two-Kay and Windgat.
- Boerassic Park is the outdoors exhibition, and to round off the vist to Evita se Perron, one can marvel at the plastic Taiwanese flora, which doesn't use any valuable water – just a duster will do.

THE KOEKSISTER

- A koeksister is a delicacy made of dough, plaited, baked in hot oil, and then dunked for a few seconds in a special sugary syrup (with a hint of lemon in it). A real koeksister should be golden-brown, crisp on the outside, and syrupy and moist on the inside.
- The koeksister is maybe the only South African delicacy that has been honoured by a monument. This monument was unveiled in Orania in 2003.
- Anna Boshoff, HF Verwoerd's daughter, unveiled the koeksister monument in Orania. It is 2 m high, and made out of polystyrene, covered by fibreglass.
- Alida Strydom and Marina du Plessis came up with the idea, and a specimen koeksister was made and sent to a sculpture foundry in Simon's Town. The first monument was rejected, because it was plaited right over left, instead of the traditional left over right.
- The monument gave rise to a huge argument about the origin of this delicacy, with descendants of Cape Town's early Malay and Indonesian inhabitants claiming it as a delicacy that their forefathers (and -mothers) had brought with them when they came to South Africa. And according to these Cape Town claimants, a real koeksister's ingredients should include ginger, coconut and nutmeg. The Cape Malay version (called koesiste) is less sweet, not twisted and covered with refined coconut.
- Another type of koesiste(r) was made with cooked potato. A Mrs Samsodien of Hanover Street invented this recipe during a time when there was a shortage of flour during the Second World War. She also added ground, dried naartjie peel for some extra flavour.

WINE IN SOUTH AFRICA

- In 1655, three years after his arrival in Table Bay, Jan van Riebeeck, the Cape's first commander, planted a vineyard, and on 2 February 1659, the first wine was made from Cape grapes. Van Riebeeck wrote in his diary: 'Today, praise the Lord, wine was pressed from Cape grapes for the first time.'

- This success led to the planting of vines on a larger scale at Boschheuvel (now known as Bishopscourt, Wynberg).
- In 1679 Simon van der Stel arrived at the Cape. He was not only enthusiastic, but very knowledgeable about viticulture and winemaking.
- He planted a vineyard on his farm Constantia and made good wine from the beginning. Constantia was later acquired by the Cloete family and their wines became world famous.
- The Dutch had almost no wine tradition, and it was only after the French Huguenots settled at the Cape between 1680 and 1690 that the wine industry began to flourish.
- In 1743 the governor-general, Baron von Imhoff, realised the quality of the grapes grown in the Cape, and recommended that wine experts come from the Rhine and France to instruct the settlers in wine-making.
- The 1793 statistics of De Mist show that the Cape had 860 000 vines, while Stellenbosch (at that time including Caledon, Paarl, Malmesbury, Piketberg, Tulbagh, Ceres and Worcester districts) had 910 000 vines.

∼ THE SOUTH AFRICAN WINE INDUSTRY ∼

- South Africa has a total area of 110 200 ha under wine grapes, with a total of more than 317 million vines. A total of 45% is under red grapes, and 55% under white grapes.
- About 350 000 people are employed both directly and indirectly in the wine industry. This includes farm labourers, workers involved in packaging, retailing and wine tourism.
- In 2003 South Africa produced 1 233 689 tons of grapes, and 956 million litres of wine, of which 712,7 million litres was good wine.
- In 2004 a total of 1 314 364 tons of grapes were produced, and the estimate for 2004 is 1 018,5 million litres of wine, of which 702,2 million litres is good wine.
- About 33% of the annual production is exported, and the other two thirds is sold locally. In 1991, 23 million litres were exported, and in 2001 it was 177 million litres; and only two years later, in 2003, this figure was 237,3 million litres.
- South Africa produces 3,1% of the world's wine, and it is the 8th largest wine producing nation.
- Most of the cultivars in South Africa originated in France and Germany, but Pinotage is a South African cultivar. It was created in 1925 by Professor AI Perold from a Hermitage (Cinsaut)–Pinot Noir crossing.
- The term 'big six', which is used in the wine industry, refers to the six so-called

noble cultivars: Cabernet Sauvignon, Pinotage, Merlot and Shiraz (red), and Chardonnay and Sauvignon Blanc (white).
- Other important cultivars are: Chenin Blanc, Riesling, Colombard, Semillon, Gewürztraminer, Bukettraube (white), and Cinsaut, Cabernet Franc, Pinot Noir, Zinfandel and Ruby Cabernet (red).
- The Stellenbosch Wine Route was the first wine route in South Africa. Wine tourism employs some 48 350 people.

∼ SOUTH AFRICA'S WINE REGIONS ∼

In 1973, with the introduction of the Wine of Origin system, South Africa's winelands were divided into a series of official regions, districts, wards and estates.

Region	District	Ward
Breede River Valley	Robertson	Agterkliphoogte, Bonnievale, Boesmansrivier, Eilandia, Hoopsrivier, Klaasvoogds, Le Chasseur, Mcgregor, Vinkrivier
	Worcester	Aan-De-Doorns, Goudini, Nuy, Scherpenheuvel, Slanghoek
	Swellendam	Buffeljags, Stormsvlei
Klein Karoo	–	Montagu, Tradouw
	Calitzdorp	
Coastal Region	Cape Point	
	–	Constantia
	Tygerberg	Durbanville
	Paarl	Franschhoek Valley, Simonsberg-Paarl, Voor-Paardeberg, Wellington
	Stellenbosch	Jonkershoek Valley, Papegaaiberg, Simonsberg-Stellenbosch, Bottelary, Devon Valley
	Darling	Groenekloof
	Swartland	Riebeekberg, Malmesbury
	Tulbagh	–
Olifants River	Lutzville Valley	Koekenaap, Spruitdrift, Vredendal
	Citrusdal Mountain	Piekenierskloof, Bamboes Bay
	Citrusdal Valley	–
–	Overberg	Walker Bay, Elgin
–	Douglas	–
–	–	Hartswater, Lower Orange, Cederberg, Ceres, Herbertsdal, Rietrivier FS, Ruiterbosch, Swartberg, Elim, Prince Albert Valley

Did you know?
- The Worcester region has the most vineyard plantings (19% of all vines), followed by Paarl and Stellenbosch (17%), Robertson (14%), Malmesbury (12%), Olifants River (9%), Orange River (9%) and Little Karoo (3%).
- The Worcester region also produces the most wine (26%), followed by Olifants River (16%), Robertson (15%), Paarl (13%), Stellenbosch (10%), Orange River (9%), Malmesbury (8%) and Little Karoo (3,9%).

WINE BOTTLES

Name	Bottles	Litres	Named after	Meaning
Piccolo[1]	¼	0,187	Piccolo – a very small flute	Italian *piccolo* – small
Demi/Filette	½	0,375	–	Latin *dimidius* – split in two, from *dis* – apart and *medius* – half; *filette* means 'little girl'
Bottle	1	0,75	–	Latin *butticila* – little cask
Magnum	2	1,50	–	Latin *magnus* – 'big'
Marie-Jeanne[1]	3	2,25	Marie-Jeanne Ozanne	She lived in the Bordeaux region in the 18th century
Jeroboam[2]	4	3,0	King of Israel	Hebrew *Yarob'am* – Let the people become great
Rehoboam	6	4,5	King of Judah	Hebrew *Rehab'am* – The nation has taken up enlarged space
Methuselah	8	6,0	Hebrew patriarch, lived to 969 years	Hebrew *Methuselah* – Man of Shelah
Salmanazar	12	9,0	Assyrian king who captured Hosea	Babylonian – Shulman is great
Balthazar	16	12,0	Babylonian king in Book of Daniel	Akkadian – Lord, protect the king
Nebuchadnezzar[1]	20	15,0	Babylonian king	Babylonian – Nabu, protect my son
Melchior	24	18,0	One of the three wise men	*Melchior* – King of light
Hendrix	32	24,0	Jimi Hendrix	American rock guitarist, singer and songwriter

1   Only used for wine bottles, not for champagne bottles.
2   Jeroboam refers to a 3 ℓ champagne bottle, but to a 4,5 ℓ wine bottle.

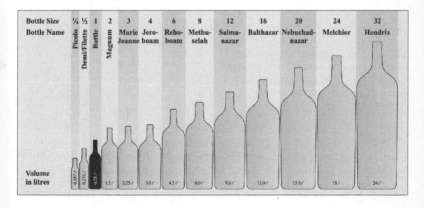

—————— SOUTH AFRICA'S TREES ——————

Arbour Week

South Africa has been celebrating Arbour* Day since 1983, more than a century since J Sterling Morton of Nebraska, USA, persuaded his local agricultural board to declare a public holiday dedicated to the planting of trees. He named his house Arbor Lodge, and within 20 years the concept of an annual Arbor Day was embraced by all the states in the USA. America's Arbor Day falls in the second week of August, while South Africa initially decided to celebrate Arbour Day in September. In 1999 it was extended to a week, called Arbour Week, which is celebrated in the first week of September. There are 2 000 indigenous tree species in South Africa. Arbour Week focuses on two tree species every year – one common and one rare species.

* Spelt 'Arbor' in the USA

∿ TREES OF THE YEAR 2000–2015 ∿

Year	Common tree English name	Common tree Afrikaans name	Common tree Latin name	Rare tree English name	Rare tree Afrikaans name	Rare tree Latin name
2000	Weeping wattle	Huilboom	*Peltophorum africanum*	Safsaf willow	Safsafwilger	*Salix mucronata*
2001	Tarwood	Teerhout	*Loxostylis alata*	Sneeze wood	Nieshout	*Ptaeroxylon obliquum*
2002	Cheesewood	Kasuur	*Pittosporum viridiflorum*	Natal flame bush	Breekhout	*Alberta magna*
2003	Red currant	Bostaaibos	*Rhus chirindensis*	Wild teak	Kiaat	*Pterocarpus angolensis*
2004	White seringa; Mountain seringa	Witsering Bergsering	*Kirkia acuminata Kirkia wilmsii*	Hiccup nut	Hikklimop	*Combretum bracteosum*
2005	False cabbage tree	Baster-kiepersol	*Schefflera umbellifera*	Baobab	Kremetart	*Adansonia digitata*
2006	Wild pomegranate	Wildegranaat	*Burchellia bubalina*	Kosi palm	Kosipalm	*Raphia australis*
2007	Common wild currant	Gewone taaibos	*Rhus pyroides*	Poison bride's bush	Gifbruidbos	*Pavetta schumanniana*
2008	Bladdernut	Swartbas	*Diospyros whyteana*	Bell bean tree	Klokkies-boontjieboom	*Markhamia zanzibarica*
2009	Tree fuchsia	Notsung	*Halleria lucida*	Round-leaved teak	Dopperkiaat	*Pterocarpus rotundifolius*
2010	Cape gardenia; Bell gardenia	Kaapse katjiepiering Klokkies-katjiepiering	*Rothmannia capensis Rothmannia globosa*	Tonga-kerrie	Tongakierie	*Cladostemon kirkii*

Year	Common tree English name	Common tree Afrikaans name	Common tree Latin name	Rare tree English name	Rare tree Afrikaans name	Rare tree Latin name
2011	Bride's bushes	Bruidsbome	Genus *Pavetta*	Common wild elder	Gewone wildevlier	*Nuxia congesta*
2012	Red beech	Rooi-boekenhout	*Protorhus longifolia*	Black mangrove	Swart-wortelboom	*Bruguiera gymnorrhiza*
2013	Crossberry	Kruisbessie	*Grewia occidentalis*	Powder-puff tree	Poeierkwas-boom	*Barringtonia racemosa*
2014	White ironwood	Witysterhout	*Vepris lanceolata*			
2015	Parsley tree	Wilde-pieterseliebos	*Heteromorpha trifoliata*			

❧ TREES OF THE YEAR 1975–1999 ❧

Year	Latin name	English name
1975	*Podocarpus*	Yellowwood species
1976	*Pinus* species	Pine trees
1977	*Celtis africana*	White stinkwood
1978	*Eucalyptus* species	Gum trees
1979	None	
1980	*Ocotea* species	Stinkwood
1981	*Acacia* species	Thorn trees
1982	*Erythrina* species	Coral trees
1983	*Rhus* species	Karee species
1984	*Ficus* species	Wild figs
1985	*Bauhinia* species	Bauhinia
1986	*Protea* species	Proteas
1987	*Cussonia* species	Cabbage trees
1988	*Olea* species	Wild olives
1989	*Calodendrum capense*	Cape chestnut
1990	*Quercus* species	Oaks
1991	*Trichilia* species	Red ashes
1992	*Dais cotinifolia*	Pompom tree
1993	*Schotia brachypetala*	Weeping boer-bean
1994	*Bolusanthus speciosus*	Tree wisteria
1995	*Combretum erythrophyllum*	River bushwillow
1996	*Warburgia salutaris*	Pepperbark
	Kiggelaria africana	Wild peach
1997	*Rapanea melanophloeos*	Cape beech
	Ziziphus rivularis	False buffalo thorn
1998	*Apodytes dimidiata*	White pear
	Greyia flanaganii	Kei beacon tree
1999	*Dombeya* species	Wild pear trees
	Cassipourea species	Onionwood trees

—————————— SOUTH AFRICAN TENNIS STARS ——————————

Major titles

The four Grand Slam (or Major) tennis tournaments are:

- The Australian Open (Melbourne)
- The French Open (Paris)
- Wimbledon (London)
- The US Open (New York)

South Africans who have won titles at these four tournaments are:

Australian Open

Men's singles

Year	Winner
1981	Johan Kriek
1982	Johan Kriek

Men's doubles

Year	Winners
1985	Christo van Rensburg (SA)/ Paul Annacone (USA)
1990	Pieter Aldrich/Danie Visser (SA)
1993	Danie Visser (SA)/Laurie Warder (Aus)
2000	Ellis Ferreira (SA)/Rick Leach (USA)

Women's doubles

Year	Winners
1959	Sandra Reynolds/ Renée Schuurman (SA)

Mixed doubles

Year	Winners
1959	Robert Mark (Aus)/Sandra Reynolds (SA)
1960	Trevor Fancutt (SA)/Jan Lehane (Aus)
1999	David Adams/Mariaan de Swardt (SA)
2001	Ellis Ferreira (SA)/Corina Morariu (USA)

French Open

Men's doubles

Year	Winners
1947	Eustace Fannin/Eric Sturgess (SA)
1972	Bob Hewitt/Frew McMillan (SA)

Women's doubles

Year	Winners
1959	Sandra Reynolds/Renée Schuurman (SA)
1961	Sandra Reynolds/Renée Schuurman (SA)
1962	Sandra Price (née Reynolds)/ Renée Schuurman (SA)
1963	Renée Schuurman (SA)/ Ann Jones (née Haydon) (VK)
1981	Ros Fairbank/Tanya Harford (SA)
1983	Ros Fairbank (SA)/Candy Reynolds (USA)

Mixed doubles

Year	Winners
1947	Eric Sturgess/Sheila Summers (née Piercy) (SA)
1949	Eric Sturgess/Sheila Summers (née Piercy) (SA)
1955	Gordon Forbes (SA)/Darlene Hard (USA)
1962	Bob Howe (Aus)/Renée Schuurman (SA)
1966	Frew McMillan/Annette van Zyl (SA)
1970	Bob Hewitt (SA)/Billie Jean King (USA)
1976	Kim Warwick (Aus)/Ilana Kloss (SA)
1979	Bob Hewitt (SA)/Wendy Turnbull (Aus)
1999	Piet Norval (SA)/Katrina Srebotnik (Slo)
2000	David Adams/Mariaan de Swardt (SA)

Wimbledon

Men's doubles

Year	Winners
1967	Bob Hewitt/Frew McMillan (SA)
1972	Bob Hewitt/Frew McMillan (SA)
1978	Bob Hewitt/Frew McMillan (SA)

Mixed doubles

Year	Winners
1928	Pat Spence (SA)/Elizabeth Ryan (USA)
1949	Eric Sturgess/Sheila Summers (SA)
1950	Eric Sturgess (SA)/Louise Brough (USA)
1977	Bob Hewitt/Greer Stevens (SA)
1978	Frew McMillan (SA)/Betty Stove (Hol)
1979	Bob Hewitt/Greer Stevens (SA)
1981	Frew McMillan (SA)/Betty Stove (Hol)
1982	Kevin Curren (SA)/Anne Smith (USA)

US Open

Men's doubles

Year	Winners
1972	Cliff Drysdale (SA)/Roger Taylor (UK)
1977	Bob Hewitt/Frew McMillan (SA)
1982	Kevin Curren (SA)/Steve Denton (USA)
1990	Pieter Aldrich/Danie Visser (SA)

Women's doubles

Year	Winners
1976	Linky Boshoff/Ilana Kloss (SA)

Mixed doubles

Year	Winners
1949	Eric Sturgess (SA)/Louise Brough (USA)
1977	Frew McMillan (SA)/Betty Stove (Hol)
1978	Frew McMillan (SA)/Betty Stove (Hol)
1979	Bob Hewitt/Greer Stevens (SA)
1981	Kevin Curren (SA)/Anne Smith (USA)
1982	Kevin Curren (SA)/Anne Smith (USA)
1994	Patrick Galbraith (USA)/Elna Reinach (SA)

THE POST OFFICE

- The SA Post Office has more than 2 000 outlets and 5 500 service points.
- The Post Office delivers 8 million mail items daily to about 6,4 million addresses – 3,4 million street addresses and 3 million postboxes.
- Speed Services Couriers move 37 tons of mail (the weight of seven African elephant bulls) EACH NIGHT!
- Seventy 50-ton container vehicles transport the mail on the country's main routes, covering 19 million km every year. The distance is equal to 475 trips around the Earth, or 24 times to the moon and back.
- The area covered is more than 1,2 million km^2 – that's as large as the total area of Austria, Belgium, France, Germany, Luxembourg, the Netherlands and Switzerland!

NAMES OF TV PROGRAMMES

Name	Language	Meaning
Takalani Sesame!	Tshivenda	Be happy!
Zama-Zama	IsiNguni	Try-Try
Bambanani	IsiNguni	Strive, struggle
Mabaleng	Sesotho	In the courtyard (i.e. on the playing field)
Laduma	IsiNguni	It thundered (the ball into the net)
Mamepe	Sesotho	Honeycombs
Lebone	Sesotho	Light/lamp
Egoli	IsiZulu	Place of Gold
Isidingo	IsiNguni	The need
Muvhango	Tshivenda	Dispute
Tseleng	Sesotho	(Born) on the roadside
Asikhulume	IsiNguni	Let's talk
Ingqumbo Yeminyanya	IsiXhosa	Wrath of the ancestors
Motswako	Sesotho	The mix (or Good stuff! in slang)
Impilo	IsiZulu	Health/life
Pasella	IsiZulu	Present/gift
Yizo Yizo	IsiZulu	This is it/the real thing
Gaz'Lam	IsiZulu	Blood that binds/brotherhood
Imvelo Yethu	IsiZulu	Our nature
Khululeka	IsiZulu	Free

PREMIER LEAGUE SOCCER TEAMS

Premier League team	Year	Home ground	Previous names	Nickname	Team colours
Ajax Cape Town	1999	Newlands Rugby Stadium	Seven Stars and Cape Town Spurs (amalgamated)	Urban Warriors	Red and White
Black Leopards	1983	Thohoyandou Stadium, Venda	Spareco Black Leopards, Sibasa Black Leopards	Lidoda Duvha	White and Gold
Bloemfontein Celtic	1969	Seisa Ramobodu Stadium Botshabelo Stadium, Zuka Baloyi Stadium, Free State Rugby Stadium	Frasers Celtic Magic Curl Celtic	Phunya Sele Sele	Green
Bush Bucks	1957	Basil Kenyon Stadium, Sisa Dukashe Stadium	Umtata Bush Bucks	Imbabala	Black and Gold
Dynamos	1997	Giyani Stadium	Lenasia Dynamos	–	Red, White trim
Jomo Cosmos	1983	Makhulong Stadium, Tembisa, Olympia Park	Highlands Park, Dion Cosmos	Ezenkosi	Red, Blue Trim
Kaizer Chiefs	1970	Ellis Park, Royal Bafokeng Stadium (Rustenburg)	Kaizer XI	Amakhosi	Gold and Black
Lamontville Golden Arrows	1996	Absa Park Stadium	–	Abafana Bes'thende	Green and Yellow

Premier League team	Year	Home ground	Previous names	Nickname	Team colours
Mamelodi Sundowns	1970	Securicor Loftus Stadium	Mamelodi United, Double Action Sundowns	The Brazilians	Yellow and Blue
Manning Rangers	1932	Chatsworth Stadium, Absa Park Stadium	Chatsworth Rangers, Ratanang	Mighty Maulers	Blue and Gold
Moroka Swallows	1947	Rand Stadium	Corrugated Rovers, Moroka Swallows Big XV	The Birds	Maroon and White
Orlando Pirates	1937	Johannesburg Stadium, PAM Brink Stadium	–	Buccaneers, The Bucs	Black and White
Santos	1982	Athlone Stadium, Green Point Stadium	Lightbody's Santos	The People's Team	Yellow with Red trim
Silver Stars	1937	Peter Mokaba Stadium, Polokwane	Mapate Silver Stars, Khakhu Fast XI	–	Black and White
SuperSport United	1985	HM Pitje Stadium, Securicor Loftus Stadium	Pretoria City, Albany City	–	Blue and White
Wits University	1922	Bidvest Stadium	–	The Students The Clever Boys	Gold and Blue

FIFA FOOTBALL WORLD CUP HOST COUNTRIES

Year	Host	Winner	Second	Score	
2010	South Africa				
2006	Germany				
2002	South Korea, Japan	Brazil	Germany	2-0	
1998	France	France	Brazil	3-0	
1994	USA	Brazil	Italy	0-0	Penalties: 3-2
1990	Italy	West Germany	Argentina	1-0	
1986	Mexico	Argentina	West Germany	3-2	
1982	Spain	Italy	West Germany	3-1	
1978	Argentina	Argentina	Holland	3-1	
1974	West Germany	West Germany	Holland	2-1	
1970	Mexico	Brazil	Italy	4-1	
1966	England	England	West Germany	4-2	
1962	Chile	Brazil	Czechoslovakia	3-1	
1958	Sweden	Brazil	Sweden	5-2	
1954	Switzerland	West Germany	Hungary	3-2	
1950	Brazil	Uruguay	Brazil	2-1	
1938	France	Italy	Hungary	4-2	
1934	Italy	Italy	Czechoslovakia	2-1	
1930	Uruguay	Uruguay	Argentina	4-2	

Did you know?

- Egypt was the first African country to take part in the Football World Cup. It was in Italy in 1934.
- Tunisia was the first African country to win a match at a World Cup tournament. It was in 1978 in Mexico, when they beat Argentina 3-1.
- Libya has never taken part in the Football World Cup.
- South Africa became a member of FIFA in 1952, and was suspended in 1964. The suspension was lifted in 1992.
- South Africa's first World Cup match was against France in 1998. Bafana Bafana lost 0-3.
- Benni McCarthy scored South Africa's first World Cup goal against Denmark in 1998.
- Bafana Bafana won their first World Cup match in 2002, when they beat Slovenia 1-0.
- South Africa has 1 500 soccer clubs, and 524 700 registered players.

———— SOUTH AFRICA'S 2010 WORLD ———— CUP STADIUMS

City	Stadium	Capacity
Johannesburg	Soccer City	98 850
	Ellis Park	64 150
Durban	Absa Stadium	64 150
Cape Town	Newlands	42 325
Bloemfontein	Free State Stadium	43 325
Kimberley	Kimberley Stadium	42 175
Nelspruit	Mbombela Stadium	43 325
Orkney	Oppenheimer Stadium	42 175
Polokwane	Peter Mokaba Stadium	42 175
Port Elizabeth	Port Elizabeth Stadium	51 825
Pretoria	Securicor Loftus	47 325
	Rainbow Junction	43 325
Rustenburg	Royal Bafokeng Sports Palace	43 325

———— THE WORLD CUP SOCCER TOURNAMENT ————

The Jules Rimet Trophy (1930–1970)

- The original FIFA World Cup trophy, which was created in 1930 by a French sculptor, Abel Lafleur, was 35 cm high and weighed about 3,8 kg.
- The statuette was made of gold-plated sterling silver and had a blue base made of lapis lazuli, a semi-precious stone.

- It depicted the Nike of Samothrace ('Winged Victory').
- There was a gold plate on each of the four sides of the base, on which were engraved the name of the trophy as well as the names of the nine winners from 1930 to 1970.
- The trophy was named after Jules Rimet in 1950.
- FIFA's vice-president, Dr Ottorino Barassi (Italy), hid the trophy in a shoebox under his bed throughout World War II, saving it from the occupying troops.
- In 1966, the cup disappeared while being displayed before the World Cup tournament in England. Pickles, a little dog, discovered it where it was buried under a tree.
- In 1970, Brazil earned the right to keep the Jules Rimet Trophy after having won the World Cup three times.
- The famous trophy was stolen again in 1983, this time in Rio de Janeiro, where the thieves apparently melted it down. The Brazilian Football Association had a replica made.

FIFA World Cup
- In 1970, FIFA commissioned a new trophy for the 10th World Cup (1974).
- A total of 53 designs from seven countries were submitted, and the winning sculptor was the Italian artist Silvio Gazzaniga.
- The new FIFA World Cup trophy is 36 cm high, made of solid 18-carat gold and weighs 4,970 kg. The base contains two layers of semiprecious malachite, and there is room for 17 small plaques for the names of the winning teams until 2038.
- The trophy cost $50 000 to make – today it is worth $10 million.
- The FIFA World Cup trophy cannot be won outright, and will remain FIFA's possession. The winning team keep it until the next tournament, and is then given a gold-plated replica.

Did you know?
- FIFA stands for *Fédération Internationale de Football Association* – the International Federation of Football Associations.
- FIFA was established on 21 May 1904 at 229 Rue Saint Honoré, Paris, by the football federations of Belgium, Denmark, France, Holland, Spain, Sweden and Switzerland.
- The Football World Cup in 2002 was the first World Cup tournament to be hosted in Asia.

- The Football World Cup in 2010 will be hosted in Africa for the first time.
- No team has ever lost its first league match and won the World Cup.
- Brazil is the only country that has participated in all the World Cups.
- The famous Pelé, or Edson Arantes do Nascimento, was the only player to win the Rimet Cup three times – in 1958, 1962 and 1970.
- The national teams of Czechoslovakia, Holland and Hungary have played in the finals twice, but they have never managed to win the title.
- No team from Africa, Central America, North America or Asia has ever won the World Cup.
- The World Cup game with the most spectators was when Brazil played Uruguay at the Maracana Stadium in 1950, when 200 000 spectators watched the game.
- The only person to have played both World Cup football and World Cup cricket was Sir Viv Richards, who represented Antigua in the Football World Cup and the West Indies in the Cricket World Cup.
- Yellow and red cards were only introduced at the 1970 World Cup.

An interesting World Cup calculation …
Before 2002, Brazil had last won the World Cup in 1994.
Before that, they had won it in 1970.
Add 1970 and 1994 – it equals 3 964.

Argentina had last won the World Cup in 1986.
Before that, they had won it in 1978.
Add 1978 and 1986, it equals … 3 964.

Germany had last won the World Cup in 1990.
Before that, they had won it in 1974.
Add 1990 and 1974, and it equals … 3 964.

For the 2002 World Cup, the sum was: 3 964 – 2002 = 1962.
The 1962 World Cup was won by Brazil.
In 2002 the World Cup was won by … Brazil.

For the 2006 World Cup, the sum is:
3 964 – 2006 = 1958
Brazil won the World Cup in 1958 …

World Cup mascots

2002	Ato, Kaz and Nik
1998	Footix
1994	Striker
1990	Ciao
1986	Pique
1982	Naranjito
1978	Gauchito
1974	Tip and Tap
1970	Juanito
1966	World Cup Willie

Recent World Cup songs

2002: 'Boom', performed by Anastacia
1998: 'La Copa de la Vida', performed by Ricky Martin
1994: 'Gloryland', performed by Daryl Hall with Sounds of Blackness
1990: 'Un'estate Italiana', performed by Edoardo Bennato and Gianna Nannini

--- SOUTH AFRICAN FESTIVALS ---

South Africa is a country of festivals, where literally every city and town, nay, even suburb, block of flats, congregation and library use the remotest possibility of an excuse to celebrate something with a festival. Some of these festivals have been around for a fair number of years; others have been included for their novelty value and/or uniqueness …

Festival	City/Town
Aloe Festival	Albertinia
Apple Festival	Uniondale
Banana Festival	Port Edward
Bastille Festival	Franschhoek
Biltong Festival	Mokopane
Bread and Beer Festival	Caledon
Calamari Festival	Plettenberg Bay
Cattle Festival	Stella
Cederberg Festival	Clanwilliam
Cheese Festival	Franschhoek/Simondium
Cherry Festival	Ficksburg
Citrus Festival	Citrusdal
Crayfish Festival	Lambert's Bay
Dias Festival	Mossel Bay
Fireworks Festival	Saldanha
Flower Festival	Elim
Fynbos Festival	Stanford

Festival	City/Town
Grape Festival	Nylstroom
Hantam Meat Festival	Calvinia
Harvest Festival	Constantia
Jacaranda Festival	Pretoria
Leipoldt Festival	Clanwilliam
Love Festival	Elim
Maize Festival	Morgenzon
Mampoer Festival	Willem Prinsloo Agricultural Museum, near Pretoria
Muscadel Festival	Montagu
Natrossie Festival [Bunch of late grapes]	De Doorns
Nouveau Wine Festival	Paarl
Olive Festival	Prince Albert; Cape Town
Ostrich Festival	Oudtshoorn
Oyster Festival	Knysna
Pineapple Festival	Hluhluwe
Play Festival	Montagu
Port Festival	Calitzdorp
Potato and Venison Festival	Petrusburg
Potato Festival	Bethal
Prickly Pear Festival	Uitenhage
Prickly Pear Festival	Willem Prinsloo Agricultural Museum, near Pretoria
Pumpkin Festival	Worcester
Rose Festival	Germiston
Rose Festival	Bloemfontein
Rose Festival	Stilfontein
Sheep Festival	Colesberg
Shell Festival	Jeffrey's Bay
Summer Festival	Plettenberg Bay
Super Splash Festival	Mossel Bay
Sweet Potato Festival	Napier
Tomato Festival	Lutzville
Van der Stel Festival	Stellenbosch
Vasco da Gama Festival	St Helena Bay
Venison Festival	Thabazimbi
Whale Festival	Hermanus
Wheat Festival	Groblersdal
Venison Festival	Mokopane
Venison Festival	Dundee
Water Sport Festival	Gariep Dam
Witblits Festival	Philippolis
Yellowtail Festival	Struisbaai

──────── SOUTH AFRICA'S WORLD RECORDS ────────

Guinness World Records acknowledges a number of world records set by South Africans:

Largest pizza
The largest pizza ever baked had a diameter of 37,4 m, and was baked at Norwood Hypermarket on 8 December 1990. It bettered the previous record, set by Pizza Hut, Singapore, in June 1990, by 3,5 m. The record pizza included 4 500 kg of flour, 90 kg salt, 1 800 kg cheese and 900 kg tomato puree.

Longest kebab
On 6 May 2000, the Dutch Reformed Church Wonderboompoort in Denyssen Avenue, Mountain View, Pretoria, made a kebab that just went on and on and on – for a whole 1 554,65 m.

Tallest Easter egg
The tallest Easter egg in history was made on 4 April 1996, by the Rotary Club of Piet Retief in KwaZulu-Natal. The 7,65-m tall marshmallow and chocolate egg was supported by an internal steel frame, and weighed 4 068 kg.

Two Booker prizes
The South African author JM Coetzee was the first person to win the Booker Prize for Fiction twice – in 1983 for *Life & Times of Michael K*, and in 1999 for *Disgrace*.

Longest salad bar
On 2 February 2002, Nola Mayonnaise made the longest continuous salad bar, which measured 201,2 m. It was at the Kyalami Exhibition and Conference Centre, Johannesburg. It weighed 2 063 kg, and contained 455 kg tomatoes, 975 kg lettuce, 375 kg cucumber, 200 kg onions ... and 58,5 kg Nola Big Squeeze salad dressing.

Most people scuba diving simultaneously
The most people scuba diving at the same time at the same place was 592. They went underwater at Vetch's Pier, Durban, on 7 July 2001, at an event organised by the Durban Underwater Club.

Largest ballet class

A total of 530 people from 41 ballet schools took an hour-long ballet class organised by the Cape Town City Ballet at the Canal Walk shopping centre near Cape Town on 12 October 2003. The dancers' ages ranged from 10 to 52 years.

Oldest competitive walker

Philip Rabinowitz of Hout Bay near Cape Town claimed the title of oldest active competitive walker, because he still regularly takes part in races over 20 km, even though he was born in February 1904 – which is more than a century ago! Rabinowitz was born in Lithuania, but emigrated to South Africa when he was 21. Rabinowitz, nicknamed 'Flying Phil', broke the world record in the 100 m for 100-year-olds on 10 July 2004 with a dash clocked at 30,89 seconds. The previous record of 36,19 seconds was held by Austria's Erwin Jaskulski. Rabinowitz recorded an even faster hand time of 28,70 seconds the previous week, but it could not be recognised because a power failure stopped the electronic clock.

Most donated blood

South Africa's Maurice Creswick has been donating blood since his 18th birthday in 1944, and donated his 336th unit of blood on 9 July 2003. That equals 188,9 ℓ of blood.

Barefoot waterskiing

Nadine de Villiers performed 17 crossings of the wake in 15 seconds at the Gauteng Waterski championships on 5 January 2001 to claim the Women's Barefoot Waterskiing Slalom Record.

Deepest freshwater cave dive

Nuno Gomes scuba-dived to a depth of 282,6 m at the Boesmansgat Cave in the Northern Cape to perform the Deepest Fresh-Water Cave Dive.

Furthest distance in a canoe

The furthest distance paddled by canoe in 24 hours was 220,69 km. Marinda Hartzenberg achieved this feat from 31 December 1990 to 1 January 1991 on Loch Logan in Bloemfontein.

Oldest English Channel swimmer

Susan Fraenkel of Cape Town became the oldest woman to swim the English Channel when she completed the swim on 24 July 1994. She was 46 years and 103 days old, and it took her 12 hours and 5 minutes.

Shortest woman
Madge Bester of Bloemfontein is the world's smallest woman. She is a tiny 65 cm short and weighs 38 kg. Her small stature is caused by osteogenesis imperfecta, a disease that is characterised by brittle bones. Her mother, Winnie, is 70 cm tall.

Most nail clippers
André Ludwick of Parys in the Free State has the most nail clippers in the world – a total of 505. His collection includes every conceivable kind of nail clipper – articulated, decorated, in silver, steel, gold plate, titanium and brushed stainless steel.

Most expensive trip
Mark Shuttleworth's trip to the International Space Station (25 April to 5 May 2002) was the most expensive tourist trip – a whopping $20 million.

Longest pizza delivery
Bernard Jordaan of Butler's Pizza in Cape Town personally delivered a pizza to Corné Krige, the Springbok captain, in Sydney, Australia, on 22 March 2001, to enter the record books for the longest pizza delivery – over a distance of 11 042 km.

Most sarcomas removed
Dr Cecil Weintraub, a doctor in Johannesburg, excised a total of 1 674 sarcomas from one person in the period from 1977 to 2001.

Travel to seven continents
Tanya Daniella Donkin, born in 1997, became the youngest person ever to have travelled to all seven continents when she visited Dubai in 2000. She was only 3 years and 319 days old. She did all her travelling accompanied by her parents, Dave and Irene.

Fastest dog weaving
Jazz, Lita Jansen's border collie, holds the world record for a dog to weave its way between 60 poles. Jazz took only 12,98 seconds to do this on 4 December 1999 in George.

SOUTH AFRICAN INVENTIONS

The people who live in South Africa have been inventors for thousands of years. The first mathematical counting device, a lunar stick found in Border Cave, Maputaland, was made about 35 000 years ago. Over the ages the early South Africans also came up with devices to make their lives easier and help them survive. They designed and manufactured bows and arrows, spears, hide shields, pottery, ploughs, fishing traps, ochre paint, ostrich shell beads, bone fish hooks and a variety of traditional medicines.

In 2004 the MTN Science Centre at Canal Walk, Cape Town, exhibited hundreds of South African inventions. A list of the 40 best South African inventions, in terms of innovation, uniqueness and impact, was compiled during the exhibition.

The 40 best SA inventions	
Invention	**Description**
Action Potential Stimulation Device (APSD)	A device for arthritis relief
Aloe vera health care products	Products made from the juice of local aloes
Appletiser and Grapetiser	Preservative-free drinks
Barlow-Wadley broadband radio	The first broadband radio in the world
Bell articulated trucks	Over 50 models sold in 80 countries
Hoodia gordonii appetite depressant	The indigenous hoodia cactus, developed by the Khoisan, is now sold worldwide
CATscanner	A major medical breakthrough for which a South African-born scientist, Allan Cormack, received the Nobel Prize for Medicine in 1979
Colindictor	The first machine in the world that could record a telephone discussion
Computicket	The first online ticket booking system in the world
Cybertracker	A hand-held database and GPS that is used by Western and traditional trackers worldwide
Dart and Flamingo sports cars	Famous for the stylish design and excellent road holding
Disa push-button telephone	The first push-button phones in the world
Vibol fuel-saving exhaust system	Reduces fuel consumption and pollution
First use of fire	One of the most significant technological innovations in the history of the human race
Fourcade's spectroscope	The first three-dimensional mapping system in the world
Freeplay radios, torches and cellphone chargers	The first wind-up appliances, which have improved the quality of life of thousands of rural people
Hippo drum and Q-drum	Large rollers or water containers that can be rolled along the ground, to transport large quantities of water with the minimum effort
Jetmaster fireplaces and braais	The advanced design has made them bestsellers in South Africa, Australia and Europe
Kreepy Krauly, Baracuda and Poolcop pool-cleaning systems	South Africa is a world leader in the design of pool-cleaning equipment
Murray 'Tour de Force' competition bicycle cranks	The first bike cranks made from carbon fibre, strong but light
Nguni and Bonsmara cattle	Selective breeding has produced cattle that are ideally suited for South African conditions

Invention	Description
Playpump roundabout water pump	Use the energy of kids playing to pump water up from the ground
Plethysmograph	The first instrument in the world for measuring rate of blood flow
Policansky fishing reels	World-class lever reels that rival Penn and other famous makes
Pratley putty	The only South African invention that has been to the moon!
Radar (pioneering innovations)	South Africans made important improvements to radar during World War II
Rooibos tea and other products	A very popular and healthy use of our floral biodiversity
Rooivalk helicopter and pilot's helmet	Lethal but innovative weapons of war
Scheffel bogie	A revolutionary railway carriage wheel system that reduced wear and tear
SharkPod shark-repellant device	Makes divers safer in our shark-infested tropical seas
Shuttle low wattage transformers	Useful and safe innovation that should be installed in every office and home
Smartlock safety syringe	Reduces the risk of infection among medical staff, especially HIV/AIDS
Smocking pleater	The first automated device for gathering and pleating clothing for smocking
Speedball (*Speedgun*)	For measuring the speed of a cricket ball, made cricket even more interesting
SUNSAT telecommunications satellite	This micro satellite has sent back superb photographs of planet Earth
Tellurometer (infrared and microwave)	A highly accurate distance-measuring device, which revolutionised surveying worldwide
Turboheat solar spiral	A new and innovative solar heater that provides hot water and room heating for rural families
Van der Bijl's pioneering vacuum tube	Used for the first transcontinental radio broadcasts, in the USA
Vuvuzela	A horn that has traditional roots and makes an awful lot of noise at soccer matches
Wadley Loop Receiver Radio	Used for radio broadcasts between South Africa and Britain

Did you know?

- Some of the more unusual inventions at the exhibition were the Madiba shirt, car tyre sandals and the Afri-Can oilcan guitar. Other 20th-century inventions include the dolos, oil-from-coal technology, developed at Sasol, the Cheetah jet fighter, the snake board, Bigboy motorised scooters, the butterfly backpack frame, Orthoped bicycle saddle and Swizzlestix canoe paddles.
- An ideal gift for those South Africans who like to braai is an outdoor picnic coaster that keeps grit and insects off the meat or wors, and shopaholics will love the unbreakable supermarket trolley.

- The Snake Board, an innovative skateboard invented in South Africa, became a huge hit internationally in 1993.
- The Snapper three-point safety plug was developed in South Africa in 1978.
- A decade later, in 1988, the high-speed tree-felling machine was also developed locally.
- Some other interesting South African inventions are:
  - A human-powered hydrofoil
  - A low-noise rock drill
  - Carbon fibre motorbike wheels
  - An automatic porridge-making machine.
- According to Proudly South African, an average of about 80 patents a month are granted by the SA Patents Office, and an average of 12 patents a month are granted by the US Patents Office to inventions originating in South Africa.

The inventors
- When unsightly cellphone masts bothered Johannesburg telecommunications engineer Ivo Lazic, he thought of disguising them as huge palm trees.
- KwaZulu-Natal's Peter Ramsay and Mark Beagle invented the world's first automatic popcorn vending machine.
- Dolosse are large concrete blocks, weighing as much as 20 tons each, which break up wave action and protect harbour walls. Eric Merrifield designed the dolos, which was first used in East London harbour.
- Sasol, the company that produced the world's first petroleum from coal, currently provides a significant amount of South Africa's petrol. (The registration letters on Sasolburg number plates were OIL, and when a second installation was built at Secunda – which means second – the letters TWO were used on the number plates).
- Somerset West inventor Henri Johnson invented the EDH Speedball in 1992, to measure the precise speed and angles of speeding objects, like cricket and tennis balls.
- Krugersdorp engineer George Pratley invented Pratley putty in the 1960s, and it was used in 1969 during Apollo XI's moon mission.
- In 1951 Ferdinand Chauvier, a hydraulics engineer, immigrated to South Africa from the Belgian Congo. He decided to take the hassle out of cleaning swimming pools, and the first Kreepy Krauly was used in 1974 at his home in Springs.
- Larry King, an Eastern Cape farmer who wanted to protect his lambs from predators, invented an adjustable collar from recycled polyethylene, to keep the dangerous beasts' vicious teeth away from his flock's vulnerable necks. The King Collar is quite popular in the USA, too, where it protects livestock from coyotes.

BIBLIOGRAPHY

∾ BOOKS ∾

Boardman, Helen. *South Africa's Top Ten Book*. Halfway House: Southern Book Publishers, 1998.

Bryden, Colin (ed.). *Mutual & Federal SA Cricket Annual 2003*. Mutual & Federal, 2003.

Burger, Delien (ed.). *South Africa Yearbook 1996*. Pretoria: South African Communication Service, 1996.

—— (ed.). *South Africa Yearbook 1997*. Pretoria: South African Communication Service, 1997.

—— (ed.). *South Africa Yearbook 1998*. Pretoria: GCIS, 1998.

—— (ed.). *South Africa Yearbook 1999*. Pretoria: GCIS, 1999.

—— (ed.). *South Africa Yearbook 2000/01*. Pretoria: GCIS, 2000.

—— (ed.). *South Africa Yearbook 2001/02*. Pretoria: GCIS, 2001.

—— (ed.). *South Africa Yearbook 2002/03*. Pretoria: GCIS, 2002.

—— (ed.). *South Africa Yearbook 2003/04*. Pretoria: GCIS, 2003.

Coastcare Factsheet Series. Pretoria: Department of Environmental Affairs and Tourism, ND.

Colquhoun, Andy. *South African Rugby Annual*. SA Rugby Pty Ltd, 2003.

Draft White Paper on Traditional Leadership and Governance. Issued by the Department of Provincial and Local Government, October 2002.

Du Plessis, M. *New Words and previously overlooked ones/Nuwe Woorde en oues wat in die slag gebly het*. Cape Town: Pharos Dictionaries/Woordeboeke, 1999.

Eksteen, LC (ed.). *Groot Woordeboek/Major Dictionary*. Cape Town: Pharos Dictionaries, 1997.

Ellefson, Connie Lockhart. *The Melting Pot Book of Baby Names*. White Hall, Virginia: Betterway Publications, Inc., 1987.

Floor, Bernal C. *Die Geskiedenis van Nasionale Paaie in Suid-Afrika*. Pretoria: Departement van Vervoer, 1985.

Folkard, Claire (ed.). *Guinness World Records 2004*. London: Guinness World Records Ltd, 2003.

Fortin, François. *Sports. The Complete Visual Reference*. Ontario: Firefly Books, 2000.

Greyling, Rosalie. *Rules of Sport* (revised edition). Cape Town: Francolin Publishers, 2004.

Heidenstam, D and S Bosanko. *Sports Comparisons*. London: Arthur Barker Limited, 1982.

Janse van Rensburg, Heila (ed.). *South Africa Yearbook 1994*. Pretoria: South African Communication Service, 1994.

—— (ed.). *South Africa Yearbook 1995*. Pretoria: South African Communication Service, 1995.

Journal of the Mountain Club of South Africa. Volume 97, 1994.

Joubert, PA. *Tweetalige Frasewoordeboek*. Kaapstad: Pharos, 1997.

Joyce, Peter (ed.). *Wêreldatlas vir Suid-Afrikaners*. Cape Town: Jonathan Ball Publishers, 2004.

Leppan, Lew. *The South African Book of Records*. Cape Town: Don Nelson, 1999.

Maclean, Gordon Lindsay. *Roberts' Birds of Southern Africa* (6th edition). Cape Town: John Voelcker Bird Book Fund, 1993.

Mandela, Nelson. *Long Walk to Freedom*. Randburg: Macdonald Purnell, 1994.

Perold, AI. 'Historical Notes on the Cape Wine Industry'. In: *The Wine Book of South Africa*. Stellenbosch: Wine and Spirit Publishers, 1936.

Raper, PE. *A Dictionary of Southern African Place Names*. Cape Town: Jonathan Ball Publishers, 1987.

Republic of South Africa: Parliamentary Register 1910–1984.

Teasdale, G and B Jennett. *LANCET (ii)* 81–83, 1974.

The Constitution of the Republic of South Africa. Johannesburg: Logos Information Systems, 1997.

Van der Elst, R. *A Guide to The Common Sea Fishes of Southern Africa*. Cape Town: Struik Publishers, 1981.

❧ WEBSITES ❧

http://dictionary.reference.com: General

http://electionresources.org: SA elections

http://learning.mweb.co.za: General (From: SA Factfile)

http://ourworld.cs.com: Grand Slam tennis results

http://whc.unesco.org/pg.cfm: World heritage sites

http://www.allmusic.com: SA musicians

http://www.anc.org.za: The ANC

http://www.anc.org.za/misc/nkosi.html: *Nkosi Sikelel' iAfrika*

http://www.aneki.com/nobel.html: Nobel Prizes

http://www.celebritywonder.com: Charlize Theron

http://www.chemistrycoach.com: Temperature scales

http://www.deltaenviro.org.za: SA environment

http://www.dwaf.gov.za: SA dams

http://www.elections.org.za: SA elections

http://www.elephantcare.org: Elephants

http://www.emporis.com: Highest buildings © Emporis Corporation 7/2004

http://www.environment.gov.za: SA environment

http://www.everestnews.com/seven.htm: Seven summits and highest mountains/Everest/ SA mountaineers

http://www.evita.co.za: Evita Bezuidenhout and family

http://www.fantasticfiction.co.uk: JM Coetzee and Nadine Gordimer

http://www.fifa.com: FIFA World Cup; Soccer

http://www.gal.co.za: Pretoria

http://www.genslin.us: Springbok rugby

http://www.geocities.com/maineiac_bibliophage/scales.html: Scientific scales

http://www.geocities.com/marcelmonterie/routelists: National roads
http://www.geoscience.org.za/seismo/historical.htm: Earthquakes
http://www.gold.org: Gold
http://www.golfweb.com/: Golf
http://www.gov.za: SA government departments
http://www.guinnessworldrecords.com: Guinness World Records
http://www.haka.co.nz: The All Black haka
http://www.hasbro.com/monopoly: Monopoly
http://www.hickoksports.com: Athletics world records
http://www.imdb.com: Charlize Theron/Oscars
http://www.info.gov.za: SA provinces
http://www.info.gov.za/symbols: SA national symbols/national orders/coat of arms
http://www.informationblast.com/: Zulu kings
http://www.iol.co.za: SA news
http://www.jimloy.com/physics: Temperature scales
http://www.jimmyspageantpage.com/sa.html: Miss South Africa
http://www.joburg.org.za: Johannesburg News Agency – Sterkfontein Caves
http://www.jse.co.za: JSE Securities Exchange
http://www.mcgoodwin.net/pages/otherbooks/nm_longwalk.html: Nelson Mandela
http://www.mil.za/Articles&Papers/Ranks: SANDF rankings
http://www.muurkrant.nl/monopoly: Monopoly South Africa
http://www.nbi.ac.za/: National Botanical Gardens
http://www.news24.com: General news
http://www.nfi.org.za: Big 12 insects
http://www.nobel.se: Nobel Prizes
http://www.nra.co.za/roadnetwork.html: National roads/Toll plazas
http://www.olympic.org: Olympic Games
http://www.oscars.com: Oscars
http://www.parks-sa.co.za: Transfrontier parks/National parks
http://www.pe.org.za: Port Elizabeth
http://www.plantzafrica.com: Trees of the Year
http://www.polity.org.za: SA national anthem
http://www.reservebank.co.za: SA Reserve Bank
http://www.robben-island.org.za: Robben Island
http://www.rock.co.za: SA musicians
http://www.sacities.net: SA cities
http://www.salt.ac.za: South Africa Large Telescope
http://www.samint.co.za: SA coins
http://www.sapo.co.za: SA Post Office

http://www.saps.gov.za/profile/rank.htm: SA police service rank structure
http://www.selftours.co.za: SA cities
http://www.sportscheduler.co.sz: SA soccer/Soccer nicknames
http://www.ssgfx.com: Glasgow Coma scale
http://www.statssa.gov.za: SA census
http://www.szgdocent.org: SA animals
http://www.taxfreegold.co.uk: Gold bars
http://www.thewaterpage.com: Water facts
http://www.turtlesa.com/Signalhill.html: Signal Hill
http://www.vep.city.victoria.bc.ca: Mercalli scale
http://www.voortrekkermon.org.za: Voortrekker Monument
http://www.weathersa.co.za: SA weather and climate
http://www.wine.co.za: Wine
http://www.women24.com: Charlize Theron
http://www.wosa.co.za/statistics.asp: Wine
http://www.wynboer.co.za: Wine
http://zar.co.za/barnard.htm: Chris Barnard

❧ ENCYCLOPAEDIAS ❧

Albertyn, CF (ed.). *Ensiklopedie van die Wêreld* (Vol. 1–12). Stellenbosch: CF Albertyn (Edms.) Beperk, 1971.

Encarta Dictionary. Microsoft® Encarta® Premium Suite 2004. Microsoft Corporation, 1993–2003.

Encarta Electronic Encyclopaedia. Microsoft® Encarta® Premium Suite 2004. Microsoft Corporation, 1993–2003.

Encyclopaedia Britannica Ultimate Reference Suite 2004 CD-ROM. Encyclopaedia Britannica Inc., 30 May 2003. Copyright © 1994–2003.

Potgieter, DJ (ed.). *Standard Encyclopaedia of South Africa (SESA).* (Vol 1–12). Cape Town: Nasou Limited, 1973.

Roos, Linda (ed.). *SAE (Suid-Afrikaanse Ensiklopedie)* (CD). Cape Town: Nasboek, 2003.

❧ NEWSPAPERS ❧

Beeld
Cape Argus
Cape Times
Die Burger
Rapport
Sunday Times

INDEX